THE

HAPPY

INTROVERT

Quirky Tales From The Depths Of Solitude

DR. NEAL B. BLAXBERG

Book design by Najdan Mancic, Iskon Design Inc.

The Happy Introvert: Quirky Tales From The Depths Of Solitude
ISBN 9781521928752

DISCLAIMER

I have tried to recreate events, locales and conversations from my memories of them. In order to maintain their anonymity, in some instances I have changed the names of individuals and places. I may also have changed some identifying characteristics and details such as physical properties, occupations and places of residence. Any likeness to similar published works is purely coincidental. The entire contents of this work are the intellectual property of the author; copyright pending.

ACKNOWLEDGEMENTS

T his work would not have been possible without the support of my Creator and Sustainer, **Hashem Yisboroch**. In fact, I would not have been possible without Him, so extra kudos on that one.

I am especially indebted to my editor, Ana Cuomo, a woman of great fealty, and many letters after her name. Thank you, Ana, for pushing me, encouraging me, and giving me that kick in the pants each day that I probably didn't need or want, but appreciate nonetheless.

I am grateful to all of the people that have inspired me to write the words, and tell the stories, that comprise the bulk of this tome.

Nobody has been more important to me in the pursuit of this project than the members of my family. I would like to thank my mom, may she live and be well, and my dad, of blessed memory, whose constant presence in my life provided me with the anchor I needed when I was going through tough times and navigating choppy seas.

Most importantly, I wish to thank my seven, amazing sons. They have provided me with the impetus to leave a lasting legacy, and I hope to spend the final third of my life rotating through their homes, so that I don't have to live on my own.

INTRODUCTION

D o you shy away from crowds? Do you shine in one-on-one encounters but shrink like a wilted daisy when the party gets busy? Do you enjoy more time alone than with others? Does your stomach start to churn and ache at the thought of having to prove your worth to yet another date, client or boss?

If you are like me, then you have many of the character traits that describe an introvert. In truth, almost no one is a pure introvert or extrovert, but many of us, myself included, fall well within the spectrum of what could easily be described, in the famous words of Greta Garbo, as the type of person who "vants to be alone!"

This is all well and good if you plan to live the life of a curmudgeonly hermit, a self-reliant pioneer, or a 'shushy' librarian who comforts him or herself by curling up with a good book, deep in the bowels of a five stories tall, big city library.

But what about those of us, again, myself included, who have chosen to engage with the world? What about career, marriage, children, and communal life? How do we reclusive types make our way in the world while still being true to ourselves?

Marcus Buckingham and Donald Clifton wrote a great book that changed my thinking about how to live life, and led me, not only to an acceptance of my introversion, but to a willingness to embrace it and see it as a source of personal power. The book, entitled, **Now, Discover Your Strengths**, delves into the particulars of character analysis, and expertly assists the reader in becoming aware of his or her unique personality traits that serve as springboards for success in the everyday world. What is unusual and promising about this work is that it strongly encourages the reader to spend the lion's share of one's time applying one's strengths to the task at hand, rather than trying (and usually failing) to make up for one's shortcomings.

From the first grade until almost my fifth decade of life, I had been trying (and failing, sometimes miserably) to overcome my weaknesses, thinking, if I just worked harder to be more outgoing, daring, willing to take risks, and unerringly direct, that I would eventually find the personal, interpersonal and professional success that I desired. Yet, despite my best efforts, with each attempt at overcoming what felt like insurmountable, internal obstacles, I found myself in a state of self-recrimination and remorse for having once again "chickened out." I could not step up to the plate of extroverted action, and my self-esteem continued to plummet along with my results.

When I figured out that I had been trying to wrestle myself to the ground, and then freed myself from such a nonsensical approach, I was able to let out a big sigh of relief, and begin the much more enjoyable task of putting my high-level life skills to work for me.

This book is for you, my introverted friend. If you have been struggling to be a shining star in your wallflower world, struggle no more. You have every tool in your own personal toolbox needed to be successful, and to fulfill your unique purpose in the world. Starting today, you can simply be yourself and let your sterling and unimpeachable introversion work for you like never before. Join me as I share with you a series of deeply personal vignettes, observations, epiphanies and ruminations that will leave you feeling exhilarated, exonerated, motivated and ready to tackle the big, bad world in your own inimitably quiet and unassuming way. Let's go!

CHAPTER 1

People erroneously believe that introverts always want to be alone. As a class A introvert, I can guarantee you that this is simply not the case. What is true about us is this: we tend to decide whether or not a social situation is working based on whether we are gaining or losing energy from the interaction.

Think about it. Have you ever been at a staff meeting, party or seminar, and suddenly felt the need to leave the room? On the flip side, have you been in a similar scenario, but felt drawn to not only staying but participating fully? Why? What was the difference between the two? If you are truly an introvert, then you will realize that it overwhelmingly has to do with whether you were drawing inspiration, support and value from the encounter, or whether you felt your life and desire leaving you like air going out of a leaky balloon.

I am very in touch with my intuitions. I remain anchored and engaged when involved in situations or encounters that breathe life into me and, concomitantly, into which I am able to breathe life. In other words, when I am interested and actively involved in an encounter, I stick around. And when I am not, either from the outset or at some point thereafter, I gather up my toys and go play somewhere else.

This sometimes requires that you "grow a pair." It takes guts to be authentic enough to get up and leave when things aren't working in your favor. Some might say to stick it out and wait for the energy to change, and you certainly have that option, but I would suggest that you ask yourself how much time you really have to spend on things that are not working. I am 56 years old. Perhaps when I was in my 20s I might have stuck around a social situation and waited to see if I was going to start feeling like I could integrate into the existing groove. At this point in my life, however, I have little or no patience for wasting that kind of time. Every moment of my life is precious, even if it is spent sitting in the parking lot of the 7-Eleven, nursing an extra-large Brazilian dark roast cup of coffee. In fact, that is exactly the setting where I came up with the idea to write this book!

When you start to become acutely aware of whether or not you are feeling inspired, involved and engaged, when you realize that your time is valuable and best spent on matters that actually matter, when you no longer feel compelled to endure what is NOT working in the hopes that at some point it will, you have entered the zone of the successful and happy introvert. Welcome!

CHAPTER 2

W hen I say the words 'small talk,' what comes to mind? If you are a hardcore introvert like me, well, to quote Jack Nicholson from *Terms of Endearment*, "I would rather stick needles in my eyes."

Introverts LOVE good conversation. A meaningful, healthy, fully engrossing exchange with another caring, feeling, intelligent human being is like a breath of fresh air, a brisk mountain hike and a Strawberry-banana-mango smoothie, all wrapped into one.

What does NOT work for us is the idle and soul-numbing chit chat that passes for dialogue these days. One scan of almost anyone's Snapchat or Facebook screen will lead the introvert to believe that everyone has lost their mind and entered a zombie-populated *Twilight Zone* of fluff and pabulum, never to return with their gray matter or typing skills intact.

It's not that introverts are effete snobs who spend their days brushing up on Keats, Shakespeare and Thoreau, nor are they attempting to master linear algebra in between episodes of *Masterpiece Theatre*. It may seem startling, but introverts have been known to peruse comic strips, occasionally window shop in touristy places, and even glance with curiosity at the Pirate Ship anchored at the local marina that takes passengers on one-hour non-alcoholic grog and "Avast ye landlubber!" cruises. But please do NOT ask us to expound on topics of insignificance; they are beneath our dignity and well below our conversational radar.

Tell us instead about an amazing encounter with an authentic self-help guru like Byron Katie or Tony Robbins. Describe with gusto the Pad Thai you ate last night, lovingly prepared in a tiny Asian take-out by a singularly gruff and unpleasant foreign chef in dirty duds. Treat us to an outtake from a Cranberries song that scrambled your emotional eggs and caused your heart to grow three sizes.

We are "feeling" people. We are folks who look to consistently and frequently recharge our 'humanity' batteries, and, as we all know, when you put a battery in a charger, it usually sits alone. Occasionally, as with the rechargeable batteries that are part and parcel of my electric razor, there is a pair, neatly analogous to the desire for the company of one other person when we are in the process of recouping our mojo. We love a cup of coffee and a deep discussion with a close friend or confidante. We cherish *tete a tetes* with those special relatives we only see at weddings and funerals but with whom it always feels like no time has passed when we are with them. And we thrive on the peaceful and stirring wisdom of nature, watching with awe as an osprey laboriously carries yet another oppressively heavy branch some ridiculous distance, just to feather its nest.

Do us a big favor and never engage us in meaningless chatter. We are not vengeful, but it could give rise to some ugliness if it persists. Whether we are alone or with others, we like to be stimulated, enlightened, entertained and turned on. And when we decide we have had enough, we check out, knowing that this, too, is for the good, as we retreat to that healthy, private space, where our juices are, once again, restored.

CHAPTER 3

I do not like crowds. I have heard it said that if a person does not like crowds, it does not necessarily mean that he or she is an introvert, but I am going to get all fundamental on this one and suggest that introverts, as a rule (which are occasionally meant to be broken), do not like crowds.

I have a terribly vivid and distinct memory of standing on line to get into a nightclub with some college friends about 40 years ago. It was a hot, humid summer night in New York City and the streets were crawling with all manner of lounge lizard, hipster and safety pin-adorned punker. As we stood on line, and as the procession inched forward, I suddenly realized that we were about to enter a small, tight, loud, crowded venue. As this inexorable reality engulfed me, I proceeded to break into a cold, clammy sweat. My stomach lurched and my brain went reptilian on me, looking for a sane and safe foothold to gain emotional and interpersonal purchase, but finding none around.

So, I did the next, best thing that came to mind, like any good introvert would do; I told my friends I was going home and that I hoped they would have fun inside that small, tight, loud, crowded descent into what felt to me like a slightly more Draconian version of Dante's ***Inferno***, accompanied by strobe lights and Day-Glo drinks.

Man, they were not happy! I mean, they were seriously bummed out! "You're not coming in with us??!! Come on, it'll be fun!" Again, all I could do was reiterate my now well-worn Jack Nicholson line and feign illness. Truth be told, I was a young and poorly developed introvert at this point, not yet conscious and aware enough to admit that my internal guidance system was sending a loud, clear signal that this was not my idea of a good time. Good, solid true friends that they were (and still are, almost 40 years later), they grudgingly agreed to accompany me home instead of going into the club, and we ended up stopping for dessert and coffee at a lovely, introvert-friendly Italian pastry shop on the way back to my apartment.

I share this so that you begin to appreciate and accept that you are not weird, strange, odd or bad if you do not like crowds. If the Italian pastry shop is your gig, go for it. Sit in the section of the library that only has one cushy chair and read awhile. Head over to that off-the-beaten-path, Korean-owned bodega and check out the assortment of kimchi that just arrived thanks to Ajima's overseas culinary connections. But for heaven's sake, get used to owning and cherishing your particular desire to be at ease, both in your own skin and in your surroundings. You will find, quite contrary to what many marketing or personal growth gurus will tell you, that these isolationist tactics will not only **NOT** ruin your chances for personal, professional and interpersonal success, but rather, will most certainly nourish the parts of you that are severely lacking in self-care, and will set the stage for all manner of creative and supportive encounters to come.

CHAPTER 4

There is this young man, mid-twenties I would say, and he makes me look rather outgoing by comparison. Although we are quite well acquainted with each other, any and all attempts on my part to converse with him fall short of the mark. He cannot seem to find an entry point in order to make his way into a dialogue with me.

This bothered me for a short while, until I spoke with a friend closer in age to me, who also knows this young man quite well. He laughed wistfully when I told him about my dilemma and responded, "Yeah, so and so only swims in the deep end." What a profound observation!

This young man has even less use for small talk than I do! He simply refuses to engage when the topic seems inane, mundane or superfluous. If I did not know him better, I might have even incorrectly labeled him as borderline autistic given his propensity to stare rather than reply. Absent an identifiable syndrome, I thought that perhaps he was a snob. I even began to doubt myself and my ability to find ways to connect with someone intelligent. All this, until I realized that he was demonstrating one of the cardinal signs of a classic introvert: an unwillingness to participate in shallow repartee.

This young man may indeed be somewhat of genius, an idiot-savant, or just a regular dude. But one thing is certain: he does not take an interest in conversation for its own sake. The topic needs to be profound, personal, relevant and meaningful. And once I took all of this into account, I was able to breathe much easier, knowing that he and I were simply operating on different planes of interpersonal existence. He was flying at a different conversational altitude than me, and that was perfectly fine.

I offer this rather extreme example because you and I will encounter thousands of people in our lives, some with whom we will click, and many with whom we will not. It will be exceedingly helpful at times like this to realize that you are okay just the way you are; and that, while a few efforts to establish a bond with another may indeed be appropriate at one time or another, struggling to find common ground, when the two of you may simply be on different wavelengths, will only sap your energy, leave you depleted, and require Herculean effort in order to reconstitute your personal reserves. Don't do that to yourself. Give your introverted inner child the benefit of the doubt when attempts at connecting with another turn into a cerebral wrestling match. Just stop. Breathe. Take a step or ten back. You are who you are. And who you are is a gift from above that no one will ever be able to replicate.

Feel better now? Good! Keep it real and keep up the great work. Two steps back can easily turn into four steps forward. We introverts do best when we take the time to appreciate when our efforts are falling short. Rather than redoubling those efforts, though, see if there is a path of lesser resistance, one that conforms more to your wavelength or altitude. Then take that path. It will probably lead you to an orchard of golden apples.

CHAPTER 5

There have been many times when I have been plopped down into the midst of a group - whether it is in a classroom, at a celebratory or memorial gathering, or especially at a casual social event - that I have experienced painful, graceless moments of not knowing what to say, or how and when to say it.

I thought for a very long time that this represented a serious shortcoming on my part. I thought that I was inept, a social bungler, or lacking in simple, conventional, verbal jousting skills. Then I realized that it ran much deeper than my initial hypothesis and found, much to my surprise, that it actually represented a hidden strength of which I had previously been unaware.

Introverts like context. We like to know what is going on before we dive into a 'give and take' of thoughts and ideas. When we happen upon a conversation that contains elements unfamiliar (or uninteresting) to us, we hesitate. Sometimes we wait a long time before chiming in. Often, we do not contribute at all. The smorgasbord on the other side of the room calls loudly.

It is not that we are stupid, bumbling or strange. It is that we are excellent listeners, **but only when we want to be**. When motivated, we eagerly gather data and try to form an outline of the jigsaw puzzle laid out before us. When we are truly involved and paying attention, we eventually feel genuinely compelled to throw our hat into the ring.

Quite often, however, the topic is not consequential or vibrant, or the company we are keeping may seem blasé. In other words, things are just not gripping enough to want to understand what's going on, and rather than come across as ignorant (one of our big fears!), we choose, instead, to keep our lips sealed.

I am not a big fan of forcing an issue. I have tried, unsuccessfully, to 'put my mind to it' and really make an effort to pay attention and acquire a good working knowledge of the particulars of a subject under discussion. Yet, more often than not, I find my mind wandering, searching for a golden goblet filled with intellectual, emotional or esoteric delight. I space out, check out, and move on, happier to leave the room and investigate the magazine stand at the hotel gift shop. I may even find something fascinating to discuss with the cashier, especially one with blue hair, chin studs, or an intriguing, low-brow fashion sense.

As Kenny Rogers would wistfully sing, "Know when to hold 'em, know when to fold 'em, know when to walk away, and know when to run." Self-awareness can rule the day if we let go of the 'shoulds' that tend to trample our psyche, and, instead, give good ear to our sense of desire. As Toucan Sam used to say, "I follow my nose!" For me, that means that I follow the smell of a good insight, a charming story, or a tasty morsel of tangy knowledge. Conversely, I tend to leave the party early (or not go at all), when I sense that my willingness to listen, grasp the topic at hand, or willingly participate, may be heavily compromised by the banal nature of the gathering or its participants. When the depth of discussion moves us to say, "Hmmm, could have had a V-8," it is indeed a good idea to shift to Plan B.

CHAPTER 6

I f you would meet me, you would have a very hard time believing that I am an introvert. I seem to be outgoing, highly garrulous, direct, assertive and openly playful. Nonetheless, I am indeed an introvert. And the reason you would think otherwise would be because you are getting an experience of me that is one-on-one, rather than one that is occurring in a group setting.

This is the deep, dark secret that the introvert holds near and dear. We love time alone, but we love precious, singular encounters with a kindred soul even more. We intuitively grasp that humans are social animals, yet our wiring is such that we are much choosier than your standard-issue extrovert when it comes to who we will talk to, and what we are willing to talk about. We easily short-circuit, and almost automatically when overwhelmed by uninvited stimuli. We like to keep it tight.

I have a distinct memory from the distant past of a favorite family friend named Lillian. Every New Year's Day, my parents (well, really, my mom!) would host a brunch for their social circle, inviting about eight or so couples of the same age and similar background to a homemade spread of salads, dips, cakes, punch and fruit. As a teenager attending these functions, I was frequently nonplussed as to how to behave. On the one hand, these were my parents' friends, not mine, so my commonality with them was minimal or absent. On the other hand, we had known each other since birth (well, my birth, anyway), so one would surmise that there was something relevant to chat about.

It would turn out that, invariably (and long before I knew I was an introvert), I would find myself at these gatherings, rather than making conversation, scrupulously observing the design on the injection-molded salmon salad, noting that my mom had expertly placed olives for eyes, carrot slivers for a mouth, a brushstroke of paprika for bodily coloring, finishing it off with a final pastiche of black sesame seeds simulating those unmistakable salmon markings. I am not artistic, nor do I really have much appreciation for decorative food design; the landscape was simply less laden with social landmines when contemplating mom's handiwork than in attempting to make small talk with groggy, dismissive adults.

Then there was Lillian; a shining star, an understated statue of grace and comportment, come to life. Lillian was different. Lillian was a Holocaust survivor. Lillian was anything but shallow. Lillian had gratitude and intelligence oozing from her pores at almost any given moment. Generous, deferential, genuine and singularly beautiful – Princess Grace with darker hair and a Czech accent – Lillian was mesmerizing. Better yet, Lillian actually seemed positively interested in what I had to say. I spoke and she listened, allowing me to ramble, yet periodically interjecting salient or poignant morsels into the exchange.

Lillian taught me early on that conversation mattered. It was not something one simply does because the setting demands it. One engages verbally with another because there is mutually derived value from the interaction. She drew me out, taught me things about myself I did not know, and helped me appreciate that there are always going to be those with whom I resonate and those who are welcome to go their merry way. I am terribly grateful to this fine woman and for the lessons learned in her company.

Find your resonance partners and give expression to the wholeness of who you are. You will delight in the feeling, and will grow tremendously from the experience.

CHAPTER 7

While it may not be a proven fact, the overwhelming evidence seems to imply that introverts need predictability and control in order to avoid finding themselves in stressful social situations.

I am reflecting this very moment on such a situation that recently occurred. I belong to a small synagogue in Baltimore. We refer to it as 'the Shtiebl,' a shtiebl being defined as someone's basement that got turned into a house of prayer. It's a decidedly homey and endearing venue, frequented largely by those who live nearby, as well as more than a few devotees of the young, magnetic Rabbi in whose house it takes up space.

As is the custom in many Orthodox synagogues around the world, I sponsored a meal following the late afternoon Sabbath service in honor of the sixth anniversary of my father's passing. Two scenarios played themselves out, one during the afternoon service itself, the other during the meal.

In each of these scenarios, I played the role of 'gabbai,' which means that I was responsible for directing traffic. During the prayer service, a small selection of attendees is called up to a large table where a Torah scroll has been opened. These attendees are then given the honor, one at a time, of making a blessing over that scroll before a small portion of it is read by an expert in the discipline. I am responsible for choosing those who will make the blessing, as well as picking out those who will remove the scroll from the security of the Holy Ark in which it is ensconced, and, finally, who will lift it up, cover it with its mantle, and put it back in its resting place when the reading is completed. In short, the orderliness and flow of the prayer service largely depends upon my ability to 'be on my game' and help things move along without a hitch.

In the second scenario, I orchestrated the logistics of the honorary meal that followed the service, from the time, two days before, when I picked out and paid for all the food that would be served, to ensuring, on the spot, that enough seats and settings were available for those in attendance, and finally, to preparing, in advance, a speech honoring my father and his accomplishments in life. Again, all went smoothly, as I did all the legwork I could do beforehand. I also managed to snag an awesome nap that Sabbath afternoon, leaving me refreshed and ready to rock when it came to the festivities.

One might think, and rightfully so, that, as an introvert, I would have either shied away from such an overt, in-your-face display of public presence. And yet, nothing could be further from the truth! I truly looked forward to participating fully in both of these religious and precious moments, and I cannot help but think that it had a great deal to do with my sense of being in control! I had a very high level of certainty that things would go well because I had carefully accounted for the majority of the details associated with each event, and that made all the difference when it came to my comfort level amongst two medium sized crowds.

When I contrast yesterday's outcomes with parallel events that were lacking both my involvement and ability to control the flow of potential outcomes, I immediately realize that my introversion often takes my feet in an entirely different direction, no matter how much I might think that I could show up and have a good time. I have bypassed numerous birthday parties, informal gatherings featuring a well-known speaker, and especially NETWORKING events, choosing instead to buy a loaf of day-old bread and feed the ducks at the pond by the cemetery, all because there were too many unknowns associated with each of the latter described scenarios.

It's food for thought. It's not scientific and it's not necessarily as broadly representative of either my own or other's experiences under similar circumstances, but I will nonetheless suggest that an introvert is at his or her best when predictability and control run high. You decide, and if you are like me, I will see you at the duck pond.

CHAPTER 8

Remember the Cindy Lauper song, "Girls Just Wanna Have Fun?" Well, it turns out that girls aren't the only ones; introverts are also big fans of the pleasure principle.

What defines pleasure for an introvert, however, is the ease with which that pleasure can be achieved. We are basic. In fact, we are so undemanding that we often disappoint others who seemingly work so hard to acquire their joy. We have exceedingly low pleasure thresholds. A glass of inexpensive (but not cheap) wine, a return of our favorite romantic comedy (or, in my case, supernatural flick) to the Netflix rotations, the smell of honeysuckle after a good downpour; all of these simple pleasures are the nectar, sustenance, and battery power all rolled into one that power the introvert's engine.

We have learned over time that the path of least resistance is often most enjoyable, if for no other reason than that it invites little expectation and virtually no possibility of disappointment. Have you ever meandered through the main square of small town on a weekend, only to find yourself harmoniously swaying to the free sounds of a local rock and roll cover band, playing for a crowd that has just happened to gather for, what you come to realize is, an anniversary celebration of the founding of the municipality? Contrast this with the sky-high price tag of a Styx reunion concert, only to discover that the band is older, slower, fatter, balder and far hoarser than you could have ever imagined.

Introverts thrive on simplicity, purity and genuine wonder. We pop up at relatively unpopulated parks, waterside walkways and makeshift farmer's markets, enjoying the sights, sounds and smells of the air, water, and food that abound.

We are sensory junkies on a yard sale diet. We love it when our eyes and ears are naturally turned on by the pristine magnificence of a waterfall, or a sunset-splashed sky with a gaping canyon as its natural backdrop. We thrill to the exquisite, olfactory tease of pit beef grilled to blackened perfection, or a mouthwatering mound of crisp French fries laced with salt and vinegar. We will NOT stand idly by while the chef places forty minutes worth of finishing touches on a watercress-infused caramel mousse. Nope. These boastful creations are way too chichi and egregiously haughty for our unadorned tastes.

When you want to know where to find good, free fun, hitch a ride (or share a cab) with an introvert. The benefit is assuredly positive and you will go to bed happier than when you woke up.

CHAPTER 9

Some introverts go to parties and some stay home. Some introverts like time together, and some like time alone. And some introverts go "Wee, Wee, Wee," all the way home.

Okay, yes, I co-opted that last line from one of my favorite childhood nursery rhymes, but when your mom recites it to you over and over for at least a year, and does it while she is counting your toes, AND makes it a point to tickle and wiggle your little, tiny, pinky toe at that penultimate moment when she recites "Wee, Wee, Wee," you, too, would have a great deal of difficulty forgetting such a brazen act of motherly love and insanity, even fifty or more years later!

The point I just tried to make, before I fell down the rabbit hole and took a psychedelic trip down memory lane, is that introverts tend to fall into a social spectrum, ranging from those who rarely go out to those who actually thrive on, and recharge from, frequent social outings. The common factor here is the need for downtime in between events. Deeply private introverts, who rarely venture forth except when necessary, fill their cup THROUGH excessive privacy; their downtime is constant and, by definition, necessary for their wellbeing. Social introverts, on the other hand, thirst for interpersonal connectivity and look with cautious and measured curiosity for opportunities to meet kindred spirits. Then, when they have had enough, the pressing desire to withdraw, recuperate and refill one's existential gas tank rears its undeniable head, and off they go seeking solace in solitude.

Then there are the rest of us who lie somewhere in the middle. There is clearly a bell curve of introversion and, as with all personality types, there exists a gamut of behaviors ranging from the aforementioned hermit-like creature, to the hilariously gregarious soul who suddenly has left the room (that would be me). Perhaps the lesson here would be to refrain from judgment when it comes to meeting someone who, at the outset, may appear like a classic introvert. Getting to know that person, along with all the nuance, texture, and subtext that accompanies most of us as we gather unto ourselves various and sundry life experiences, will produce a wealth of information and allow us to see the totality of the individual, rather than view him or her through the parochial lens of prejudice and pre-definition.

In fact, I hereby suggest that we utilize this methodology when it comes to meeting ANYONE and EVERYONE. All of us have met someone that, at the start, seemed like this or that type of two-dimensional persona. Yet, when we delved deeper, and withheld judgment, either for some time or for always, we got to know a fascinating, uncommon and startlingly complex human being, rather than some caricature that we may have devised due to our own limited thinking. Take the challenge today. See each other in the newest, imaginable light possible, and watch as a gratifying sense of appreciation and acceptance comes your way.

CHAPTER 10

I have a coaching client, we'll call him Fred. Fred is a computer programmer and a weekend musician. Fred loves both time alone and time together with friends, probably in equal amounts. What Fred does NOT love is carrying out certain tasks that tend to be tedious, stuffy or risky. Now, we're not talking about an offer to go bungie-jumping (which he may indeed enjoy; personally, I would rather die a horrible, slow death from ingesting an excess of *egg foo yung* than ever undertake such a venture), nor are we discussing the particulars of picking a song to play on the jukebox when all the offerings predate our parents' first wedding anniversary.

We are talking about things like getting caught up on back taxes or calling an insurance company to get a health insurance quote because we let our COBRA coverage lapse. These onerous tasks have something in common that introverts, as a rule, would rather avoid: Uncertainty.

Introverts like small to medium-sized menus. Too many choices can cause overwhelm. They like to know the options before making a decision. Given the choice of heading out in mid-winter to one of two YMCAs with heated, indoor swimming pools, one of which writes the water temperature for that day in BIG, PINK chalk accompanied by an avuncular, anthropomorphic 'sunshine-y' face, or the other that makes you wait until you arrive, hit the locker room, change, and then head out to the pool area and stick your toe in the water to gauge further willingness, can you guess which pool the introvert will choose?

Introverts can appear, on the surface, to be perfectly normal when it comes to social (and even non-social) intercourse, and that is largely because they have surveyed the goings-on beforehand. They know exactly what they are getting into, and they will even jump in head first, and without pause, because they know and are overtly comfortable, and at ease, with the milieu. But show them a hefty pile of bank statements, point out that they bounced eleven checks last month, and then demand that they balance that darn thing before they even eat another meal; well, they would just as soon starve as tackle such an unwieldy, cumbersome, and soul-deadening task.

Organization and the ability to confront situations, social or otherwise, depend a great deal on whether one tends toward introversion, in large part due to this sense of disability and deflation that overtakes an introvert at the mention of such a situation's urgency and need for resolution.

Notwithstanding all that was just discussed, and putting the case of Fred aside, there are LOTS of introverts out there who are both extremely organized and who enjoy tackling an unwieldy pile of family heirlooms requiring sorting and distribution to the next of kin. If they can properly survey the inventory and match it up with that article's deserving recipient, the average introvert will jump at such an opportunity. It not only stokes his or her sense of accomplishment, but also, more importantly, allows for that vital and nourishing 'alone' time.

Complicate the matter by throwing in a few monkey wrenches, however, and you will have blown that poor introvert's circuits. Make him or her choose between a government subsidized health plan that is less expensive, but involves a great deal more red tape vs. a self-funded, non-subsidized plan that is costly but efficient, and you will most likely find that introvert skulking away to the safety and sanctuary of his man-cave for more than a few rounds of online poker.

Predictability, a sense of personal satisfaction, accomplishment, and simplicity, are the calling cards of the garden variety introvert. Providing him or her with options that literally reek of said characteristics will make you a veritable hero in that introvert's book. And you can take that to the bank; just make sure it's a bank located on a main drag and offers user-friendly online access.

CHAPTER 11

I am thoughtful. I was not, however, always thoughtful. I was not particularly thoughtless, heartless or careless, but I was clearly not as thoughtful in the past as I am now.

Perhaps it has to do with raising my seven beautiful boys, or going out of my way to remain civil – even friendly – with my three ex-wives. It may have a great deal to do with becoming a religious man in my late thirties, a habit I have managed to sustain and develop over the twenty years since doing so.

I would like to pat myself on the back and tell you that I really had to struggle to overcome my inner desire to remain selfish, self-centered, aloof and uncaring. But the truth is that I honestly believe that my basic nature is one of thoughtfulness; I just needed a little manicuring of the soul to flesh it out, refine it, and become adept at applying it. In short, I was a thoughtful diamond in the rough and I am getting better at it each and every day.

And so, it is with introverts.

We are thoughtful people. We get along well with the few (and sometimes many) in our inner circle with whom we choose to interact, work, play, and whose company we find enjoyable, engaging and inspiring. We make decent bosses, excellent co-workers and (three ex-wives notwithstanding) can often be some of the most loving spouses you will ever find.

We look for ways to be helpful to others. We go out of our way to choose the better Hallmark card, one that speaks more to the heart and less to the funny bone. We choose topics on which to dialogue that are of keen interest to the other parties involved. We aim to please, yet are rarely sycophantic or co-dependent, as we do not have the patience to spend that kind of energy pleasing people who are undeserving of our attention and affection.

Whether we are narrowing down the birthday party invitation list, paring down the data needed for a Power Point presentation, or deciding which floral design will work best at a cotillion, we always seek to get inside the mind of the one or many involved, hoping that our willingness to please and tailor the details to the participants will lead to a good time had by all.

So, while it may, indeed, be true that a dog is a man's best friend, even more axiomatic is that thoughtfulness and introversion are the peanut butter and jelly of the interpersonal universe.

CHAPTER 12

My second wife was, and is, a self-admitted exercise junkie. She starts her workout at 5:30am (notice I did not say GETS UP at 5:30am; she is actually AT the gym at that unholy hour), then puts herself through the paces of everything from aerobics to weight training to yoga, returning home in a nick of time to feed our youngest son his breakfast, and hop a quick shower before getting him off to carpool at quarter past eight.

She will teach yoga classes throughout the rest of the day, going through each of the positions, motions and poses with her students, often offering back-to-back sessions for a variety of women with differing schedules, then wrapping up her evening with a personal training demo for a prospective weight loss or fitness client. In short, the girl likes to sweat.

And what do I do in order to maintain my lean, lithe, lanky 6'2", 180 lb. frame? Well…I walk.

Yep. I walk. Mainly, I walk my dog, Yodi. That's the dog's name. It's a cross between Yoda, the short, green *Star Wars* sage from outer space, and Odie, the dumb canine who always seems to be at the butt-end of a Garfield prank. It was impossible to go with one versus the other because Yodi is typically either THAT smart or THAT dumb, depending on the hour, weather or squirrel in question.

Introverts REALLY enjoy walking. We derive tremendous benefit from it. We commune with nature, watch the leaves change with the seasons, notice plant and animal life that most people overlook or fail to appreciate in the hustle and bustle of the rat race, and generally feel like we are accomplishing a feat that is both good for us and enjoyable at the same time.

Aerobics class? Nah. Weights? Too heavy! Team sports? Puleez.

We thrive on the perfect storm of alone time, sensory stimulation, and the bonding of man or woman with his or her Source. There is just nothing that defines an introvert like walking. In fact, if there was an Introvert Olympics, the only sport would be walking and I would be a gold medalist.

When you want to make friends with an introvert, suggest a walk. Wait! Did someone ask "Wanna go for a walk??" Sorry, gotta run! I mean, walk! Bye!

CHAPTER 13

A bout twenty years ago, I made a monumental decision resulting in a radical life change. Virtually overnight, I decided to become religious. Specifically, I decided to become an observant Jew.

I was born Jewish and raised in a traditional Jewish home, but sought greener pastures (or so I thought), both secular and spiritual in nature, when I reached an age at which I began to question the tenets of my upbringing. At various times, I explored what it was like to be a punk rock DJ, with its attendant attire and culture; a New Age seeker, meditating to the pre-recorded chants of a California guru; and a chiropractic fundamentalist, espousing and pontificating on the distinctions between vitalistic and mechanistic health doctrine.

Throughout these journeys, I kept my banal, worldly pursuits on a short and accessible leash; if and when I felt disappointed at having, once again, chosen a pointless or tiresome path, when I felt stuck and lacking a weekend revelry outlet, I would have a number of familiar fallbacks at my disposal. I almost always went out on Friday night, and on most Saturday nights as well, nursing that carefully cultivated set of bruises, that hangover, or that pseudo-spiritual high for as long as its flavor, crunch, and texture might last.

There was one big problem: I did NOT enjoy these weekend nights out. I always felt out of place, uncomfortable, distant and removed from whatever was going on around me. It wasn't exactly that my sophomoric pursuits left me wanting; indeed, there were moments when I felt very alive and vibrant, whether it during was a brief slam-dancing encounter, an exuberant, happy hour joke telling contest, or a group share at a Twelve Steps retreat. The problem was bigger; my inner compass wanted to keep pointing me toward one of two destinations, neither of which was on the map I had opened up and consulted; it wanted me to either connect with one interesting person and spend the evening discussing something significant, or to go find a peaceful nook and read a good book. Partying left me drained, spent and cranky. My compass and I were at odds.

Then, a magical thing happened. It's quite a tale; but for our purposes, the short version will do.

At a certain point in time, I was married to my second wife, had one son from a prior marriage, and two from the current one. My concern for my children's intellectual, emotional and spiritual well-being was starting to create blips on my mental radar screen, mainly stemming from a disastrous, yet somehow divinely orchestrated PTA meeting at my oldest son's elementary school. I came home from that meeting scratching my head and wondering how either my child or I were going to survive twelve years of stultifying, soul-numbing, secular education!

As we all know, the emphasis in these hallowed public-school halls is placed squarely on the shoulders of reading, writing and 'rithmetic. After-school activities essentially come down to Little League or the glee club. The common thread here is that NO emphasis, whatsoever, was placed on personal development. This is – and rightfully so – left to the family to fill in the gaps. Values and morals are generally not taught in public schools.

I was simultaneously awakening to the importance of nascent spirituality in my own life, in my marriage, and in the lives of my children, and public school seemed at odds with the desire to inculcate such a mindset in my children. Quite to the contrary, I foresaw that, were my child to spend five days each week, seven hours each day, for a goodly portion of the year, in such an environment, the chances that he would grow to become a 'mensch' (Hebrew for 'a good person who does good things') were slim to none.

I was caught between a rock and a very hard place. I had left my past behind; there was no lingering desire to take up where my unfulfilling Jewish life had left off twenty-five years prior. My wife was seemingly satisfied with visiting the Hindu ashram and communing with her guru, but even she admitted that her approach might be too lofty an undertaking for a child. We needed a unifying element. And one showed up in a most unexpected form, delivered straight from the mouth of Dr. Laura Schlessinger.

Most of you have heard of 'Dr. Laura,' as she is commonly known, but in case you have been living under a rock since the '90s, Dr. Laura is a radio talk-show host who solves people's moral dilemmas in three minutes or less. She is brash, takes no backtalk, and gets straight to the heart of the matter each time, cutting through layers of caller confusion like a sushi knife through high-grade tuna and bringing clarity to the topic at hand.

My encounter with destiny occurred one summer day when I was thirsting for a good rock and roll song on FM radio, on the way home from work (punk rock DJ, remember?). When I could not find a single, acceptable, head-banging ditty, I flipped over to AM radio instead, hoping for an engaging, conservative, talk show rant. Instead, I tuned in to Dr. Laura.

It so happens that, at this particular time in her life, Dr. Laura was undergoing a conversion to Jewish Orthodoxy. She was not born Jewish, but eventually came to appreciate that morals and values largely stem from the Hebrew Bible, and she thus took it upon herself to pursue this approach and bring it to its logical, practical, religious conclusion.

The caller of the moment was complaining that she and her spouse were of different religions, and that it was creating tension at home, especially as it pertained to the upbringing of the children. It was creating many childrearing issues (Xmas or Chanukah? Circumcision or christening? Bar mitzvah or altar boy?), and was contributing to a general breakdown in family dynamics, all because of this 'mixed marriage.'

Dr. Laura made no bones about it, opining that three things must be in place before one can begin to raise physically, emotionally and spiritually healthy, well-adjusted children. First, there must be religion in the home; second, the parents must share the same religion; and third, the religion that is practiced should be that into which the parents were born.

This was an absolute revelation for me! Here I sat, ill at ease but nonetheless resigned to my and my wife's differing and incomplete approaches to personal and spiritual growth; yet, at the same time, fully aware that none of what we had to offer could work for our children. This presented a huge dilemma that had to be solved, and solved quickly, for the following reason; there is one very big thing that my now ex-wife and I fully agree on to this day: We want and wanted to raise happy, healthy, value-driven children.

So, we became religious. We got rid of all the non-kosher food in the house, bought new dishes, cutlery, pots and pans, phased out television and moved to a neighborhood teeming with yarmulke- and wig-adorned religious folks. And we became one of them.

You MUST be wondering what ANY of this has to do with introversion. Thank you for going along for the ride. The punch line is imminent.

Remember when I said that Friday and Saturday nights were disappointing? That no matter how much I and my wife tried to make the secular, social scene work, we were always left wanting? The religious approach for us turned that entire reality on its head!

We suddenly found ourselves, instead of sitting with popcorn and unrealistic expectations at the movies on Friday night, sharing a Sabbath meal with neighbors. We were having REAL conversations about things that mattered, with people we grew to know, connect with, and love. We shared values. We shared stories. We shared backgrounds. We shared lineage. We shared.

Our existence went from cotton candy to caviar in a blink. We were now living the wonderful, wild, wacky and meaningful world of TRUE INTROVERTS. All the pieces had fallen into place.

I had felt like a square peg trying to occupy a round hole for so very long. With the advent of our new lifestyle, I suddenly felt a lightness of being that was, and is, deeply satisfying. I was home. I was at peace. I was living a life that mattered.

Now, lest you think this is some sales pitch to try out religion, well, I leave that entirely up to you. I am only suggesting that, from an introvert's standpoint, I genuinely hoped and prayed for relief from the upset and discomfort that came from trying to stuff my introverted self into a non-introverted casing. My religious shift, the community in which I found myself, the people with whom I began to associate, and the framework within which my life began to evolve, caused every part of my introverted being to shiver with delight and resonance.

So, there you have it. Go figure out what kind of life fits your introverted profile. It will probably be one that includes quiet time, a peaceful sanctuary, meaningful relationships, genuine conversation, thoughtful reading, sensual satisfaction and a layered, textured, nuanced connection with your family.

Or you can go out to a nightclub on Friday night. Good luck with that.

CHAPTER 14

I have been accused, rightly so, of choosing option C when offered A or B. I am an 'outside the box' thinker, and so are most introverts.

I was a chiropractor for almost thirty years, but work-related injuries eventually put the kibosh on my manipulative methodologies. I was more than 50 years old when this occurred, and, like many middle-aged folks, was faced with an excruciating dilemma: I was far too young to retire, but way too lazy (just being honest) to go back to school and take a bunch of courses in order to figure out what I wanted to be when I grew up.

I stewed about this for quite a while. I waffled, vacillated, and made deals with myself about how I was going to proceed. I half-heartedly searched online for positions with universities as some kind of health education instructor (I did, after all, have nine years of health-related education and almost thirty years of health care experience under my belt). I also toyed with the notion of becoming a motivational speaker on topics concerning health and wellness, but ultimately spent a generous portion of my time ignoring the whole kit and caboodle, choosing, instead, to walk my dog, whip up new versions of a few of my favorite Korean noodle dishes, and largely avoiding all things called J-O-B.

My avoidant tendencies revolved mainly around the word 'job' itself. In my decades of chiropractic practice, I never once felt like I was going to 'work,' nor that I had a 'job.' Chiropractic was much more a calling than a profession. I was not alone in thinking this way; ask any chiropractor and you will hear much the same thing. Now that I was essentially unemployed, however, I needed to conjure up the same 'outside the box' mentality that had taken hold of me more than thirty years prior, and begin to visualize what form of gainful employment would neatly conform to my introverted, 'I'm on a mission,' worldview.

I want to share with all of you a neat little exercise I invented after coming across a few helpful ideas when I Googled "What do chiropractors do for a living after they stop being chiropractors?" (yes, I actually Googled things like that every day). In this exercise, I divided a piece of paper into three columns, placing a heading at the top of each one. The first one read, 'THINGS I AM GOOD AT,' the second one read, 'THINGS I ENJOY DOING,' and the third one read, 'THINGS THAT MAKE MY LIFE MEANINGFUL AND PURPOSEFUL.'

Once I had completed this part of the exercise, well, I went and took a nap, because that alone felt like a lot of work. When I woke up, I next took about three to five minutes and made a list under each of those headings of different kinds of activities that corresponded to that category. For example, I listed 'cooking,' 'teaching,' and 'entertaining my kids,' under 'THINGS I AM GOOD AT.' I then listed things like 'walking the dog', 'making Pad Thai', and 'helping people feel better', under 'THINGS I ENJOY DOING.' Finally, I threw down such thoughts as 'acquiring and sharing wisdom,' 'eating for better health,' and 'role modeling' under 'THINGS THAT MAKE MY LIFE MEANINGFUL AND PURPOSEFUL.' There were quite a few more listings in each column, but you get the idea.

The final step was to sit back and review what I had listed in each column, cross-referencing items in one column with those in the others, and, ultimately, discerning where these areas overlapped. The nexus of that overlap became the foundation and basis for my next step in the workaday world.

If you cannot guess where the overlaps lay, I will give you a hint: it has a lot to do with relationships, speaking, writing and advising. In short, I became a life coach!

I honestly do not believe that I would ever, in a million years, have come up with this idea on my own if I had sat down, followed the rules, and tried very hard to solve the puzzle of taking my next step. Fortunately, my introverted, 'outside the box' antennae were working well that day. Discovering the life coaching niche was as familiar as sliding my feet into a perfectly, well-worn pair of old slippers. It satisfied all my needs for income and, most importantly, gave me that 'one-on-one,' 'let's talk about stuff that matters,' template that my reticent, circumspect and 'I could never work a 9 to 5 job,' introverted persona could so easily master and deliver.

Your introversion may, at times, seem like a pesky albatross around your neck (or a monkey on your back if you prefer primate analogies over avian metaphors), limiting social inclusion, and driving you to seek out dark and dank catacombs in which to bolster and nurture your privacy. I am going to boldly suggest, however, that you can and should become best friends and buddies with your introversion; partner with it, listen to it, respect it, come to depend on it, and, when you most need it, you will find that it will deliver that 'outside the box' solution you crave.

CHAPTER 15

I have a dirty little secret. I keep it under tights wraps, largely because, as an introvert, I don't have that many friends to begin with, and if this secret were to get out, I would probably have to move to the Magdalene Islands, off the coast of northeastern Canada. I don't speak Welsh all that well, and they speak a lot of it there, so I am only going to tell you, but I need to trust that you will file it away under the heading, "Dr. Neal's soft underbelly." Are you ready? Are you sitting down?

I like to watch professional wrestling.

Not collegiate wrestling. Not Sumo wrestling. Not Olympic-style, Greco-Roman wrestling. I am talking about men in tights. Hulk Hogan. Ric Flair. Duane 'The Rock' Johnson. The Undertaker. Bobo Brazil.

You have probably never heard of Bobo Brazil, and you may not be all that familiar with the other characters mentioned heretofore. That would be because, unlike me, you spent your time more wisely on Saturday afternoon when you were twelve years old, playing stickball or jumping rope, instead of sitting in front of a rabbit-ear antennae, black and white television set, watching grown men grunt and fume as they tossed each other around in what is commonly known as 'the squared circle.'

Most people do not acquire a vocabulary that includes terms like 'hammerlock,' 'pile-driver,' or 'Swanton bomb.' The overwhelmingly majority of civilized human beings do not hope to see a 300 lb., sweaty behemoth draw blood from his opponent's forehead, utilizing a makeshift boxcutter as a carving device. Rarely do cultured, well adjusted, refined ladies, gentleman and children chant 'LOSER' at high volume and in unison at the bad guy, as he vainly attempts to shout them down, hurling a volley of invectives back at this feverish mass of rabid fans, all of whom are hoping to see the good guy demolish his dastardly opponent.

For those of us, however, who vicariously thrill to the sound of bodies hitting the mat from a well-choreographed elbow smash or devastating body slam, there is almost nothing that rivals professional wrestling when it comes to cheap (or free), cheesy and lurid, yet largely kosher, entertainment.

Introverts love wrestling. Oh, yes, we do. We pop our microwave popcorn, invite the dog up on the sofa for a few pats and a puffy kernel or two, keep a good book nearby in case the match of the moment gets tedious or features less than stellar talent, and off we trot, merrily, eagerly, and willingly, into the land of grappling intrigue and mayhem.

What do introverts love so much about this parody, one so over the top in its predetermined outcome, that it is not even legally allowed to be called a sport? After all, not only do we know and accept that it is fake, but, having watched it on and off for decades, can predict the story lines long before they happen, calling the shots way in advance, much like the crowd at the 2,345[th] screening of *The Rocky Horror Picture Show,* shouting, "What have you done to Brad?!"

Ah, but unlike that twisted, rock and roll tribute to Frankenstein in drag, we do NOT have to endure the wrenching discomfort and uneasiness of waiting in line, tolerating others' obnoxious, loud, cringe-worthy behavior, sitting in old, moldy, ergonomically crippling theater seats, or feeling our gorge rise from the sickly-sweet odor of a gargantuan box of strawberry-flavored Twizzlers that is long past its expiration date.

Not us! We LOVE our den (or living room, or bedroom, or wherever we turn on the Tube). It is quiet, cozy, and climate controlled. The only odors impacting our olfactory apparatus are the ones we choose to generate or create. Moreover, we are in complete control of the beginning, middle, and end of our suplex-infested interlude, thanks to the wonders of YouTube and various technological advances that allow us to revel on demand, in our time, when and where we decide to seek out such guilty pleasure.

If you are a die-hard wrestling fan like me, then you will appreciate the following quote from Stuart Chase; "For those who believe, no proof is necessary. For those who don't, no explanation will do." I would love to continue to chat but I am feeling an urge to go see what John Cena is planning in his return match with Brock Lesnar. Have a great time at Rocky Horror. I will be waiting with disinfectant when you get home.

CHAPTER 16

I recently finished reading a very unusual book, entitled ***The Stranger in the Woods: The Extraordinary Story of the Last True Hermit*** by Michael Finkel. It details the remarkable story of Chris Knight, a self-described misanthrope, who left civilization one sunny afternoon and secluded himself in the woods of central Maine for twenty-seven years.

Twenty-seven years! During this time, he spoke to no one, including himself. He managed to survive on petty pilfering of local vacation properties in the area, never leaving an effective footprint from which to track his hidden whereabouts. His thievery included such items as: a mattress, flashlights, a camping stove, batteries, clothes, shoes, coats, hats, gloves, blankets, a radio, multiple wristwatches, tarps, cooking utensils, books, magazines, toiletries, OTC medicines and a LOT of food. He spent a great deal of time lost in thought, ate, did laundry in a local stream, and read every stolen book and magazine that he had swiped, cover to cover.

I will leave the rest of the story to your pursuit, but I bring it here as a stark example of introversion gone wild. This fellow, from the earliest age, found himself to be his own best company, preferring to avoid social interaction whenever possible, and restricting himself to activities and endeavors that could best be done solo.

In general, introverts are simply nowhere near this extreme. Most of us crave a modicum of human connectivity, and will poke our heads out, and even exit our shells, in search of friendly discourse, if, and when, the mood strikes. It tends not to strike with nearly the frequency or regularity that it does the extrovert, and it usually has limits and exclusions that come directly from our introvert's playbook: short, deep, meaningful, engaging and life-affirming exchanges are a requirement. Without these, well, the Maine woods look inviting.

In 2015, I fulfilled an almost 20 year-long 'bucket list' dream. In 1996, I had the pleasure of vacationing on a tiny island in the Caribbean. Vieques, an island municipality of Puerto Rico, lies six miles off the east coast of the big island. It has no traffic lights, no chain stores or hotels, little or no nightlife to speak of, enchanting, deserted beaches, and an unsparing smattering of wild ponies and Brahman bulls, wandering its fields, jungles and, often, its streets in search of snacks, treats and impressionable tourists like me. One might find oneself returning from a midnight stroll on a secluded, oceanfront promenade, only to end up at standstill in the middle of a two-lane byway, as a small but hefty herd of four-legged, tropical oxen meander at a seemingly snail-like pace across the only stretch of road between you and your rented hacienda. It is paradise, with a whiff of manure.

When I visited in 1996, I went with my wife, two children, and a nanny, and spent a great deal of time with a couple of similar age and background with whom we had connected on the Internet and who had family on the island. It was blissful, sandy, sunny, yet not totally relaxing, as the obligations incumbent on young parents – even with a nanny present – would frequently intrude.

Not the case in 2015! Recently divorced, and with most of my seven progenies having reached the age of reasonable self-sufficiency, I kenneled my pooch, stopped my mail, gave my clients the heads up that I was incognito for a bit, and headed back to 'La Isla Nena.'

I will not tease you with the florid details of my temporary abandonment of all things civilized. Suffice it to say that it satisfied my need to revisit a locale that held a special place in my heart. It did not, however, fill the contents of my introverted basket with all the required goodies for which I had hoped.

Indeed, it gave me fairly large swaths of alone time. Certainly, I was intrigued, entranced and often engulfed by the natural beauty of the abundant, and lush, plant and sea life. Even the people were decidedly friendly and helpful. So, what was lacking that left me somewhat dispirited after several days and wanting the trip to be over?

It turns out that the very things that our erstwhile hermit, Chris Knight, sought in the wilds of Maine – seclusion, exclusion, privacy and social deprivation – are not the exclusive or rightful domain of the introvert. They fit more aptly into the category of 'greatest solitarian of all time.'

Introverts are rarely, if ever, hermits. We genuinely enjoy human touch, connection, warmth and exchange. We just like doing it on our terms, and typically in far smaller quantities than most. We micro-brew our social affairs.

We tend to wither, however, when we go too long without intimate banter; it's the watering can that gets emptied in measured quantities when we sense our interpersonal leaves getting droopy. We are not monks or ascetics, aching from a deep, inner place to withdraw in order to re-establish our sense of balance in the world. We like ourselves and we like others. We just don't like too much of a good thing.

I left Vieques with no regrets. I had revisited an idyllic retreat I once considered pretty darn close to perfect. But I realized, in retrospect, that one of the things that had made it so enjoyable the first time around had been the presence of newfound friends and existing family. When I went back alone, there was no easy way to recreate that vibe, and all the bougainvillea and dolphin sightings in the world were not going to be an acceptable substitute. Just as man does not live by bread alone, introverts draw sustenance from more than just pretty scenery.

CHAPTER 17

There are awkward moments in life, there are painfully awkward moments in life, and then there are moments that are so excruciatingly awkward that crawling into a hole and chanting 'I'm not really here, I'm not really here, I'm not really here,' does little or nothing to remove that creepy-crawly feeling of unbounded horror, and that falls far short of silencing that unhinged, inner voice that screams "RUN AWAY!"

Extroverts are experts at either confronting or ignoring awkward moments. Some even seem to relish their appearance, diving in like a foodie at an all-you-can-eat Sunday afternoon Chinese buffet. But for the introvert, awkward moments rank right up there with the dry heaves or a root canal when it comes to the question, "Where would I rather be right now? The obvious answer is, "Oh, that's right! ANY place else!"

My most vivid memory, by far, of THE most awkward moment in my entire life – and I must emphasize that, while I have had many, what I am about to share is not hyperbole – occurred during my sophomore year in college, when I dutifully assumed the role of lab assistant in the environment psychology department at a prestigious mid-Atlantic university.

A little background is in order. I was pre-med at the time and was looking to boost my visibility when it came time to apply to medical schools.

Since many of them like to see student involvement in extra-curricular pursuits, I thought it wise to put the little spare time I had to good use, so I volunteered to inject mouse brains with toxic aluminum salts. Yes, the mice were alive. No, they did not squeak all that much when I did it. The goal was to inject them repeatedly over a period of weeks, then cut their cute little heads off, and examine their freshly excised brains for evidence of degenerative changes caused by aluminum infiltration.

For the few and the proud among you who actually get into this stuff, the purpose of the experiment was to gather data pertaining to aluminum ingestion and its effects on brain form and function. Aluminum has long been suspected of contributing to that wonderfully dismal condition known as Alzheimer's disease, as well as other forms of dementia and brain damage, so we were not just sacrificing mice; we were seeking to protect humans from the mortal dangers of this metallic monster.

Unfortunately, I never got to see the fruits of my labor. In fact, there were no fruits. And the reason there were no fruits is because somebody forgot to feed and water the mice on the days when they weren't getting aluminum injected into their teensy brains. That would have been the other five days of the week, since the injections were only administered on Monday and Thursday. That someone, who 'forgot,' was me.

Because these experimental rodents were receiving only about 35% of the food and water they needed to survive, the little critters valiantly fought their basic instincts for as long as they could, but finally gave in and summarily cannibalized each other. Yup, that's right, the bigger ones ate the smaller ones, until the only one left was the king of the mountain, Big Bubba Mouse. And, boy, was Bubba BIG.

I was fired as soon as my immediate superior found out what had happened. He was really mad. Steaming mad. And, being somewhat of a vengeful type, he decided that it was not enough to let me know by phone or in private that I had been canned. No, he was much more bent on magnificent reprisal. He waited. He waited until he managed to catch me in the most compromised state imaginable. He accosted me in a very public setting, while I was humbly and lazily working as a part-time landscaper on the college grounds-keeping team. He waited for the opportune moment, caught me completely off guard during a lull in the drone of the cicadas, and pounced on me in front of a whole crowd of lettered professors, students and fellow employees, most of who knew me quite well, and shouted, in true Donald Trump style, "YOU'RE FIRED!"

I had never felt so small in my twenty-odd years of existence. More to the point, I never realized just how much I HATED being the center of attention, especially when that bullseye was laced with arsenic. It almost compared to the time a rival of mine for an eighth-grade girl's attention got hold of my diary (yes, I kept a diary; some boys actually do that, and do not necessarily grow up to become 'different'), and read it over the loudspeaker, to the entire school. Suffice it to say that its contents contained some revealing dirt about my unbridled desire to hold this girl in my arms and offer her my undying devotion. Actually, it was a bit cruder than that. You get the idea. I was mortified.

Being fired in public eclipsed even this, probably because the stakes were infinitely higher. My future career had been rear-ended and towed to the junkyard. I sat on the curb for quite a while, staring at the fuselage of my now overturned aspirations, and only after some time did I manage to cobble together a reasonable plan B. Truly, were it not for this event, I may have ended up a dermatologist instead of a chiropractor. Let it be known, therefore, that all of you back pain sufferers that I helped over the years have aluminum-injected mice to thank for derailing my original work-related, intentions and choosing manipulative medicine as my calling, instead.

In retrospect, I sometimes still wonder if introverts become introverted because they experienced galvanizing situations that caused them to draw inward, or, alternately, that they tend to behave in an introverted fashion when confronted with awful and embarrassing circumstances because they were wired that way from the outset. I'm not a scientist, so I am going to leave that decision to the experts. I can, however, tell you this, and I can say it with authority: Introverts do NOT like the uninvited limelight. As a rule, we are happier in the shade, eager and ready to jump on that gravy train that whispers to us in gentle and unassuming ways. We will work with you and help you accomplish great things. All we ask is that you offer us fair recompense, give us a decent footnote, and, whatever you have planned, PLEASE DO NOT put us in the difficult or disturbing position of having to explain to a large audience why we are so darn good at what we do. Just leave well enough alone and allow us our quiet victories.

CHAPTER 18

I do not think I am going out on a limb when I posit that introverts possess a high degree of emotional intelligence. The Google dictionary defines emotional intelligence as '**the capacity to be aware of, control, and express one's emotions, and to handle interpersonal relationships judiciously and empathetically.**'

This is not to say that extroverts fail miserably at exhibiting emotional intelligence; it's just that introverts spend more time in their heads, contemplating the nature and complexity of their and other's emotional landscapes. Only when we have focused our lens on another's senses and sensibilities, and have taken an accounting of the benefits and risks of getting involved with them, do we then give ourselves the green light and make a move that signals the desire for discourse.

It was such a relief to discover this about myself some years back! In the past, I would judge myself quite harshly, finding all manner of incriminating evidence to prove to myself that I was a social misfit. Why did I have so much trouble opening up in a room full of familiar faces? Why did I feel like the odd man out at weddings, bar mitzvahs and graduation ceremonies? Why did I pay much closer attention to the titles on book spines contained in the glass-enclosed, library cabinet than to my classmates' nametags when attending my thirty fifth high school reunion?

It's really quite simple. I, like many introverts, hate being caught with my pants down. What if I incorrectly identify the face in front of me, broach an uncomfortable topic, or sit next to a complete boor and end up being dragged through the evening, having to endure a monologue on the joys of Ham radio? Unlike the extrovert, who would most likely look at these hypothetical story lines as opportunities to 'network' (I hate that word), introverts would sooner volunteer to have bamboo slivers inserted under their fingernails, like those used to extract confessions from the enemy, then ever submit to the indignity of having to embrace or endure any of the above described scenarios.

We are circumspect specimens. We like to know exactly who and what we are getting involved with, and in. We are measured in our choices, conserving and reserving our energy and excitement for those people, and those moments, when there is a high probability of maximum impact and effect. We are the original economists, saving up our precious and valuable emotional and relational currency for worthwhile purchases.

One of my favorite people in the world is my friend, Yonatan. An Israeli native, Yonatan came to America – and specifically Baltimore – to seek out a religious life. How ironic! Yonatan grew up in the middle of Jerusalem, surrounded by the cream of the religious crop, but only donned devotional garb and attitude after a visit to the States and a serendipitous encounter with a five-foot-tall, giant of man, Rumi Cohn. Rumi's story is worth a book of its own, and indeed there is one on the bookstore shelf, but suffice it to say that Rumi's charisma and dedication to a sanctified life led Yonatan down a holy - and wholly unexpected - path.

I met Yonatan in the summer of 2016. As the '*gabbai*' (Hebrew for 'director of traffic') of my local *shtiebl* (Hebrew for 'basement synagogue'), I make it a point to search out new adherents who radiate warmth, participatory interest, and an unquenchable thirst for spiritual growth and meaning. Yonatan fit this bill to a 'T.' His genuine smile, penetrating gaze, measured manner of speech, dignified carriage, and humble visage made him an immediate and desirable target for friendship and camaraderie in my book.

Yonatan meets all my requirements for interpersonal rapprochement; he is personable, deep, an excellent listener, an engaging conversationalist, and, perhaps, best of all, extremely sensitive and deferential to the nuances of my moodiness. We have become best friends over a very short period of time, and I am truly grateful for his presence in my life.

As an emotionally intelligent introvert, I pick and choose my friends more carefully than I do my children's pediatrician. I can conscience an aloof allopath (as long as they know how to vaccinate in five seconds or less), but I have shied away from more potential friendships than an arachnophobe avoiding cobweb-infested cellars. I would rather spend time alone than be beaten over the head with the humdrum or mundane. If Yonatan remains one of my few friends for life, I am at peace. I need little, but expect much. How about you?

CHAPTER 19

When you think about where to go on vacation, does Disneyworld appear at the top of the list? Does it even make the list? If your personal makeup includes even a small percentage of introversion, Disneyworld would be as far from a choice of holiday spot as lettuce is to a lion's diet.

For that matter, would you venture into the heart of Africa and go on a safari? Would you sign up for one of those all-inclusive, Jamaican resorts? Do you have any desire to visit thirty European cities in thirty days?

Yeah, me neither.

Introverts do indeed enjoy a week or two away, lest you come to believe that we are homebodies who rarely if ever venture beyond our domestic comfort zone. The key, however, in being able to label it as an actual 'vacation,' is to settle on a destination that offers us that unique and winning combination of modesty and 'homey'-ness, without actually spending time at home.

We like to settle in. We often preview our travel choices and make the decision where to go and stay based on that location's ability to cater to our laid-back and pseudo-reclusive needs. We will often rent a home or villa, rather than stay at a hotel, preferring a place with a recognizable kitchen, a decent size bathroom (without a phone!), and an actual deck or patio that affords us the opportunity to chill and grill, without having to dodge questions from well-intentioned but nosy strangers.

We enjoy ritual. Eating if, and when, the chance arises is anathema to our sense of renewal. We like a nutritious, attractive breakfast, a quick and easy lunch, and a leisurely, romantic dinner. A quick, greasy snack shack or a raucous, rowdy bar will leave us cold and cranky.

We like quiet, preferring pastoral to urban settings when travelling. Noise upsets us. We're also not particularly fond of ice cream-sticky children's hands invading our mutually shared space. When feeling unusually energized and even a bit frisky, we will sometimes opt for a day-long sojourn into the busy heart of an appealing and inviting town, city or beach area nearby, but will always leave the option open to withdraw and return to the safety of our temporary fortress of solitude when an iota of overwhelm begins to surface.

We really appreciate a home away from home containing a well-stocked library! Give us some sunscreen, a comfortable lounge chair, a pool with a waterfall, and a copy of the latest New York Times Book Review #1 Bestseller, and we are happier than a pig in the mud. Well, an erudite pig, anyway.

Introverts are creatures of habit. As such, we view the words 'travel' and 'travail' as variations on the same theme. We endure the thought of leaving the peace and tranquility of our nest in order to ensure that we continually broaden our horizons. We embark on journeys that promise true rejuvenation, the possibility for growth and personal expansion, and upon which we are able to capably navigate unfamiliar highways and byways without undue stress or strain. Learning to drive on the opposite side of the road in Bermuda is a BAD idea.

The friendships we form when away often last a lifetime. I believe this is, in large part, due to our tendency to be very picky regarding with whom we meet and speak. Moreover, The Law of Attraction often leads us to connect and resonate with kindred souls, i.e., with those folks who, like us, tend to seek out a level of discourse that can contribute to a strong and lasting bond between parties.

I wish you much rest and relaxation the next time you take time away. Even more, I truly hope that your experiences will be ones that enrich and enhance your ability and desire to live life more fully upon your return. Bon voyage!

CHAPTER 20

I s it nature or nurture? Diathesis or stress? Inborn or acquired? There are many names for the split in opinion on whether introversion, or its counterpoint, is something that is predetermined, or whether it develops as a result of our experiences and involvement in the world.

I do not believe that we need to take sides on this issue; rather, one could easily make the argument for a blend of the two. Just as men and women each contain a complement of classically masculine and feminine behaviors – some men exhibiting compliancy, some women behaving in a more overtly forward manner – so, too, there are those of us who demonstrate, early on, a strong tendency toward isolation and reticence; others want to get 'into the mix' and often stop at nothing to accomplish this feat.

If you have read this book in order, you already know that I lead a religious life. If one wanted to observe introversion vs. extroversion in action, one need only spend a few hours attending a Jewish house of worship. I imagine this to be true in other religious settings as well, but I can only speak to my milieu. It was in my 'shtiebl,' (basement synagogue) one Saturday (Sabbath) morning, that I was privileged to observe this remarkable phenomenon.

A little background is first in order. My 'shtiebl' is set up in the basement of my Rabbi's home. It is narrow and long, with the cabinet ('Aron Kadesh') containing the holy Torah scrolls emplaced at the eastern end, or front, of the room. Chairs and tables for members occupy the two sides of the room throughout its length, until one reaches the back table, at the western end of the basement, where a 'Kiddush' (devotional snack session) is held after Sabbath morning services.

It does not take a rocket scientist to quickly note that the introverts sit toward the back of the room, the extroverts toward the front. The shy, recessive types shun both participation and attention, aside from adding their presence, which is often required to ensure that enough men (ten, or more) are gathered to form the Jewish version of a quorum, known as a 'minyan.' I am the exception in this sectarian setup. I sit toward the front, as I enjoy basking in the warmth of the Rabbi's presence (he's a shiny, happy, spiritual guy; he also sits up front). I like to stand close enough to the person leading the service (the 'Ba'al Tefillah') in order to be able to hear what is being said, chanted or sung. In general, though, the introverts in our congregation do not seem to derive pleasure from active involvement in the various prayers, preferring, instead, to stay out of the limelight, satisfied with being counted toward the requisite number of participants.

Not so as regards the adorable, young, side curl-sporting, Chassidic imp that showed up on this particular Sabbath morning in question! As I was attempting to orchestrate the proceedings, I became aware that I had a helper who was not of my own asking. This bespectacled lad merrily inserted himself into the order of the service, directing traffic as it were, and doing his best to either accompany or usurp the person of the moment in his role. Whether someone was being asked to lead the service, was honored with an opportunity to have a portion of the Torah chanted on his behalf, or was asked to lift and cover the Torah scroll after we were done reading it, this little, gregarious gremlin was at the ready to lend a hand, or simply be the hand in place of the hand that was designated for that current assignment! Only after the boy's father gently, but firmly, informed his son that it was someone else's turn, did the boy grudgingly step down and, once again, assume the role of observer. And that lasted about fifteen seconds, after which time the tyke was off again, happily attempting to pre-empt another's participatory efforts.

Nobody really minded this little guy's intrusiveness; most, in fact, including myself, found it rather endearing. A few, again including myself, felt a tinge of envy that someone so young could insinuate himself without a shred of self-consciousness, into the affair of the moment. It seemed to me to be a testament to the innate tendency toward extroversion.

If we flip the kaleidoscope around, however, it is quite possible to look through the other end of it and appreciate quite the opposite perspective.

One of my sons, fourth in the birth order, was quite shy and uninvolved in social matters until his teens. A late bloomer physically and emotionally, he would most often choose activities and environments more suited to a budding island castaway. I can attest that he spent the better part of two years wholly enveloped by a pair of headphones. He had successfully tuned out all that was unrelated or unnecessary to his ongoing need for food, clothing or shelter.

Then, without warning, around the age of sixteen, he started exercising, grew muscles that I genuinely never believed were possible given his father's lack of Herculean endowment, and became active in all type and manner of social proposition, even going so far as to become the president and leader of quite a few clubs and youth organizations, in and out of school.

Why did this ostensibly introverted kid suddenly switch gears, literally flipping himself inside-out in such a short period of time? Was it his physical development, lacking when young, that became more prominent, dominant and manifest as his years increased, that led to the onset of his now, highly outgoing demeanor? Did he find himself overshadowed by several older brothers (and a mildly, overbearing dad) when younger, only allowing himself to shine when he broke free of these confines? Was it there all the time, but I was too wrapped up in my own concerns to notice it?

Again, I am no scientist, so I will leave the analysis to the experts. Moreover, this is a treatise that is highly anecdotal and makes no attempt to summarize or draw definite, irrefutable conclusions. To be sure, I enjoy asking the questions more than diving deeply into the material to find the answers.

And that may be the crux of this chapter. We started out asking about the probability of introversion, or its opposite, having its roots in some DNA-influenced pattern, versus developing through a series of life events that guide its evolution; but at the end of the day, we get what we get. The lesson, at least for me, is being able to extract meaning, value and a set of tools for being, and becoming, from this admixture. It is hoped that these skills, strengths and talents will ultimately drive us to seek out a life where we will experience peace, joy, and purpose, all while remaining aligned with our truest nature.

CHAPTER 21

I pack more into a day, week or month than most. That's no small feat, given that I am semi-retired. My day begins before 6:00am and ends around 11:30pm. Within the confines of that interval, I wake, shower, shave, walk the dog, spend an hour in prayer at the synagogue, pour over a juicy piece of Scriptural commentary, take my teenager to school or camp, drive for Lyft, grab breakfast at my favorite bagel shop, check and return emails, write, do my banking (both online and at the branch), run errands, take a stroll, keep an eye on my investments, walk the dog (again), oversee the marketing of my handful of businesses, coach a few clients, engage in afternoon prayer, pick up my son from school or camp, shop for and cook dinner, power nap, meet my youngest son at the bus stop, serve a meal, join in a Scriptural study session, do homework with the boys, walk the dog (yet again), check on my tenants and their well-being, teach a class at my 'shtiebl,' join in the evening prayers, make my punch list for the following day, walk the dog (one last time), read, and go to bed. In my free moments, I try to connect, by phone, with my five sons, who no longer live at home, play with my dog, chat with close friends, say hello to my mom in Florida, do a little exercise, play with my weekly menu options, catch up on professional wrestling news, throw down a Facebook challenge to someone's easily-offended sensibilities and, when the opportunity arises, have a heart to heart with my Rabbi.

The above is not a display of braggadocio. It is my day, pure and simple. It is pretty much the same thing most every day, because I cherish order and predictability. Sudden shifts in the above-described pattern make my tummy ache. What is most peculiar about my above-mentioned routine, though, is that it almost always allows for large swaths of down time, where I am either doing almost nothing, blissfully spacing out, brainstorming strategies for world peace, or simply trying to figure out why the dog barfed up the same puppy treat this morning that he was able to keep down the day before.

I despise chaos. I loathe a packed social schedule. And I glorify free time, as it gives my mind a chance to happily stumble upon ideas and action steps that light up my creativity buttons.

I am an introvert extraordinaire, as uneasily quantified as your average millionaire, religious personality or dairy farmer, because there is no such thing as average when it comes to any of these categories, and even more so when it comes to my own.

Notwithstanding that last statement, introverts clearly have a number of things in common. We are often (but not always) happier alone, drained by forced, social engagement, love unfettered time and the activities that allow for it, and cringe at the thought of having to live up to some artificial standard of societal *savoir faire*.

We like to create, derive or establish our own standards. We often revel in taking the road less traveled (as long as the bathrooms at the rest stations are modern and clean). We delight in oddball encounters with eccentric people or out-of-the-way destinations. More than this, we need an oversized dose of recharging, at frequent intervals, and are easily depleted by the demands of a conformist world. We are the classic square peg, warily avoiding all the round holes on the planet's physical and spiritual surface. In short, we don't fit a mold.

There are those, like myself, who are energized by a day filled with numerous, soul-soothing activities and contrivances. Then there are those who would sooner donate a kidney than tackle the laundry list of things I listed above, and that comprise the bulk of my average day. They would prefer, instead, to have few, or no, obligations other than what pays the bills and offers gentle inspiration. There are those who seek frequent calm and decompression, while there is more than a sprinkling who effortlessly and gladly lose themselves in a Times Square, rush-hour crowd, happily window shopping or inhaling the intoxicating scent of those expertly blackened, yet still soft, salty, street vendor's pretzels.

We are indeed a diverse bunch, distinctly different and remarkably similar. We have little difficulty recognizing each other in a crowded room, although, to be honest, we don't go into those types of rooms all that much. We are content (or are learning how to be so) with our lot, happily ignorant of the rat race and its entry requirements. We didn't give up. We just never chose to jump in. We like it on the sidelines. A quiet locker room, in fact, is even better. You'll find us where you are not. Think about that.

CHAPTER 22

My brother is almost nine years older than me. A successful attorney and medium-level real estate mogul in Florida, he toggles between high pressure litigation in Miami and drywall repair near Tampa. On the one hand, it seems to balance out on paper; on the other hand, it sounds similar to placing your feet in the oven, your head in the freezer, and declaring yourself comfortable 'on average.' It's not my idea of a good time, but it seems to work for him.

I owe my brother a debt of gratitude for many things, but one thing in particular comes to mind, an event that changed the course of my life in more ways than I can count. When I was nine years old, my brother taught me how to ride a bicycle, without the training wheels.

Back in the 1960s, I was the proud owner of a Schwinn Stingray. There were other brands on the market – Fuji, Raleigh, and Motobecane come to mind - but these other makes were considered peripheral, inferior or immaterial in suburbia (even though they may have actually been constructed of better materials) to the more well-marketed, American-made brand. Along with a slew of neighborhood kids, I spent endless hours cruising up and down my block, happily whiling away the spring afternoons and entire days of summer, without a care in the world.

I nicknamed my bike "Goldie." Goldie had a blue frame, an elongated, golden banana seat (hence the moniker), and a garish, high-back, sissy bar extending upward, in an awkward, but passable, pre-pubescent attempt to convey my 'don't mess with Blaxy,' testosterone-fueled image.

My image, however, suffered terribly from the dreaded, appended, 'training wheels,' firmly affixed to the rear axle of my primary mode of transport. It made me look like the uncoordinated and incapable oddity on the block, shown up by numerous kids much younger, braver and sassier. I tried to hold my head high and I pedaled mightily along the same streets as my peers, but was often reminded, in rather unkind ways of my insufficiency. Juveniles, even the non-delinquent kind, can be mean.

All that came to abrupt end, one day, when my brother decided that, at nine years of age, I was overdue for a two-wheeled experience. His heart was in the right place; he genuinely wanted me to fit in with the other boys and girls, and was visibly perturbed that his younger brother was the lone geek. Taking the bull by the horns – or in this case, the Stingray by the sissy bar – he made it his mission to end my reign of ignominy, and afford me a newfound sense of pride, freedom and adventure.

Leading me outside to the driveway one bright summer morning, my brother wheeled my bike out from the garage and told me to 'saddle up.' I paused, then hesitated, then vigorously balked at the request, noticing that something crucial had gone missing from my beloved Goldie – the training wheels! How was I to proceed? What had changed, since the day before, that would afford me the balance or skill to accomplish this impossible feat? It felt like I was being asked, unrehearsed, to accompany Karl Wallenda on a tightrope walk across the Grand Canyon. NO CAN DO.

My brother was, and is, a big, strong guy. He is not used to taking "No" for an answer and is rarely deterred from achieving a goal. Without skipping a beat, he INSTRUCTED me to get on the bike, stabilizing it by holding firmly to the sissy bar, and counting to ten, while I got the feel of having lost my safety net. Then he leaned over, and whispered in my ear a few choices words, the likes of which remain with me to this day, some fifty years later. I kid you not; the hairs still stand up on the back of my neck when I recount them. He said (or, more accurately, hissed), "I am going to give you a push. And you are going to ride to the end of the street. And if you don't, I am going to KILL YOU." He didn't crack a smile. He didn't give me a moment to consider my options. He simply gave a firm and furious push. And I rode!

I rode like the wind! I rode like a storm-chaser trying to outrun a vengeful twister. I rode like Alfalfa, fleeing the scene of an indiscretion with Darla, desperate to avoid the ire of Butch. I rode like my life depended on it, for, indeed, at that moment, it most certainly felt as if it did!

When you toss a pebble into a still pond, the ripples extend, endlessly, outward. Once I was given the gift of mastering the art of two-wheeled cycling, I went on to greater and greater heights, first daring to leave the street and risk the greater beyond (the next block down held unseen wonders), then venturing outside of the neighborhood, then sallying forth and departing the town I grew up in, if only for the day. My spirit soared with each new vista visited, and outpost inspected.

My bicycling career culminated, at the age of 21, as a group leader (a paid position, no less!), of a 500 mile-long hosteling and camping trip; a tour that took our rat pack up the Hudson River valley, starting out in New York City and ending in Montreal, all under the auspices of American Youth Hostels, Inc. During this trip, I was responsible for the safety and care of ten adolescents, only six years my junior. We made it there and home in one piece, and the feather in my cap for this accomplishment was plucked from the plumage of my brothers' determined and decisive wings.

Bicycling is to introversion as a hand is to a glove. There is absolutely no need to interact with anyone or anything beyond one's natural surroundings when traversing a fifty mile stretch of backroad through the Vermont countryside. Brief stops for snacks and hydration lend themselves beautifully to the introvert's urge to connect with that interesting couple that owns and operates the general store, or the family who invites the group over to their Winnebago-populated campsite for marshmallows and hot dogs, handily blackened over a campfire. These marvelous and unscripted occasions filled my introverted cup with the liquor of pure bliss. You'll hear more about my bicycling antics a few short chapters from now; this segment is an abbreviated version, as it functions better as an ode to my sibling.

If my brother is reading this, I want to thank him publicly. He was uniquely instrumental in adding a compelling element to my repertoire of solitary habits. I treasure that gift each day. May we each add another brightly colored feather to our splendorous, introverted caps as we courageously forge our way through this glorious life.

CHAPTER 23

I am the proud father of seven, amazing boys. I've been doing the 'dad' thing for quite some time; so long, in fact, that more than half of those boys now qualify as men. I watched (not too closely, mind you) as they exited their mother's womb, changed THOUSANDS of diapers, lovingly wiped spit-up off of mom's shoulder (when she forgot to throw a cloth over it before burping them), marveled as they learned to crawl, walk and run, and generally lost a mountain of sleep, worrying myself to a frazzle about each one's spiritual, emotional, and physical well-being.

And can you believe it? They are all fine. Ten fingers and ten toes remain mostly intact, facial features are recognizable, albeit having metamorphosed from puppy to dog (as all of us are wont to do), and each one seems capable of simultaneously walking, talking and chewing gum. It's remarkable; all that anxiety and so little return on the investment. I will definitely know better the next time around.

What beguiles me is how, so early in each one's life, an easily recognizable, personality pattern emerged. One boy is the affable, thoughtful, reticent one, like his dad. Another is a 'walk (and speak) softly but carry a big stick' type, and yet a third is as outgoing, gregarious and comfortable in crowds as a Three-card Monte shyster when working his Times Square audience.

I posed the nature versus nurture question in a previous chapter, but, after reading what I just wrote, am heavily inclined to suggest that introverted and extroverted tendencies emit powerful whiffs of pre-determination. I would be hard-pressed to deny the influence of our upbringing, culture, or social stratum on our disposition, but after watching these kids of mine grow into super-sized portrayals of the pint-size renditions of old, I 'lean toward the genes.'

I would even go far as to say that we are formatted to turn out one way, or the other, but that galvanizing moments can cause the pendulum to swing wildly, resulting in a far less flexible version of that malleable one that existed only in embryonic form up until that point; or, alternately, upsetting the apple cart so definitively, leaving the hapless victim in a fugue state, wondering and wandering aimlessly as he or she seeks to re-establish some degree of, previously reliable, firmness.

Let me share a case in point.

I was skinny, shy and more than a bit goofy growing up. I didn't play too many boy games, largely because I was risking serious bodily harm were I to have done so. My mom spent a lot on braces and I was neurotically attached to keeping all my teeth, both straight and as a full set.

Then I hit puberty. My hormones started raging, girls started to look appealing, and my parents' demonstrations of protectiveness became overbearing. I needed space; space to become me, to individuate, to actualize and grow into the man I hoped to become. Mostly, though, I needed the space to sneak off to the food court at the mall, by myself, and order a tostada and a non-alcoholic beer at Fiesta Hut without having to explain my choices.

Standing between me and a trip to that food court was a lack of transportation. Although I could certainly ride my bike, that would only be possible during the daylight hours; once darkness set in, the roads and their lack of bike lanes (these had not been invented yet) made it treacherous to embark on the three-mile journey from home to Hacienda. I was forced to rely on my mom and dad for a ride to and fro, and of course, this included their company. Yippee!

To make matters infinitely worse, Dad liked to keep all the kids, and especially me, on a short leash. He accomplished this feat by the use of his favorite, shiny, shrill police whistle. When I would venture too far from his purview, a blast would go forth, followed by the intrusive and unmistakable 'voice of DAD,' overheard shouting "NEAL, WHERE'D YOU RUN OFF TO??"

I had run off to find the nearest hole that was big enough to swallow me up.

Growing up in a relatively small town where a large percentage of Friday night, mall-going, diversion-seekers knew each other by face and name, all would turn and stare directly at me when 'the call' would go out. Crimson became my natural, enduring complexion; withdrawal my default setting.

I was already an awkward, bookish, hesitant nerd. I was rapidly developing into a full-fledged candidate for the advanced study of library science. HOWEVER, I did hang out with a few cool kids and had a handful of genuine, 'join the masses' interests such as concert attendance, roller skating, and intramural basketball, all of which could have eventually assisted me in transforming my halting demeanor into something more outgoing.

The police whistle in the mall ended all of that.

I suggest that all of you well meaning, hovering, 'helicopter' parents back off. Give your kid some space to figure out his station in life. Do NOT smother him with odious doses of safety, security, and shielding. He is not a snowflake; he will not melt. Nor is he like Gumby, so twisty and malleable, standing no chance of self-realization, when pitted against the contorting elements of today's society. He's already on this way to becoming his own person. For Pete's sake, just give him some rope.

And donate the police whistle. There's a crossing guard working tirelessly at a Hanoi intersection who could really use it.

CHAPTER 24

L ife coaching is my current occupation. I could not dream up a better profession for an introvert, for the following reasons. I work when I want to work. There is no clock to punch, or co-workers with whom I must co-exist. The water cooler conversation is usually between me and my dog, Yodi, in between, before, or after clients. I dress in dorky duds, and drink cup after cup of homemade coffee, until I have trouble typing due to caffeine-induced tremors; then I switch to water.

I rarely answer the door when the bell rings; whoever is there can leave the package or the notice. I take frequent walks ALONE, between clients, or toast a bagel, do laundry, or do whatever the heck comes to mind, which is quite a lot of stuff, because I ALWAYS have something I could be doing. The best part of it all is that I get to do all that stuff if, and when, I want, and not according to someone else's notion of how to be a responsible adult.

Now, lest you come to think that I am oafish, lazy, unmotivated or slovenly, I am here to tell you that nothing could be further from the truth. I am impeccable about my appearance, I am neat and clean, and I am a bona-fide expert in seeing to it that my many obligations and commitments are fulfilled. The thing is, I try to keep them limited to those things that matter.

Which brings us to the crux of what may make an introverted life (and any other kind of life, for that matter) a happy one.

Let me ask you a question: Do you choose your obligations and commitments, or do they choose you? In other words, are you consciously and actively handpicking your life circumstances, or are you a passive bystander, waiting for life to come your way, and only then trying to figure out what to do with the cards you've been dealt? You may never have given this question much thought, and may, therefore, have a poor understanding of the difference between the two approaches. Perhaps an example of each will shed light on the distinction.

There are those folks who meekly await — and, only then, deal with - life's challenges, trials and tribulations, passively and indiscreetly allowing people and events to invade their space, uninvited. Only when the smoke has cleared and the dust has been shaken off will this individual assess whether, or how, to respond. More often than not, he will simply stand there, like a deer in the headlights, wondering why he is, yet again, a victim of circumstance.

Imagine showing up for work with no clue about what type of task you are going to be asked to do that day, where and how you are going to be expected to do it, how long you will need to do it for, or when and how you will actually know that it is done. Are you exhausted just thinking about where you fit into this **Buckaroo Banzai** parody? Are you expecting to have a rewarding day, or are you simply hoping that you don't drown in a sinkhole of office-induced muck and mire? Are you sneaking swigs from the flask hidden in your blazer pocket, rather than confidently sipping your Starbucks Double Caramel Latte, bemusedly dabbing at your whipped cream mustache with your napkin?

Although this scenario may sound ludicrous, it is not uncommon for many people to orchestrate their lives according to this set of rules (or lack thereof). They show up, say "Hit me with your best shot!" and then hope for some improbable, unlikely, benign - or even positive(!) - outcome. I think a nice, relaxed round of Russian roulette would be preferable.

Contrast the above described maelstrom with the following approach.

At night, and as you wind down with a nice Shiraz or Merlot (with overtones of oak and currant, of course), you dedicate a certain amount of time to contemplating how you would like to spend the upcoming day, arriving at a complement of activities that work to nourish your body, mind, and soul. This could easily include a form of gainful employment or other money-making enterprise, as most of us like to eat. This part of the day is necessary, yet, in the life of one who is dedicated to both predictable and optimal outcomes, this segment also tends to be neatly compartmentalized, as there are other equally important components to living a balanced, satisfying and meaningful life, aside from work. When you do finally retire (to bed, not from 40 years of 9 to 5), you feel at ease, buoyant, and expectant, knowing that you have lined up your ducks in such a way that the day to come will prove to be an adventure.

This, in my humble opinion, defines and outlines the path for success in life and living. It is, however, a generic formulation. Specificity comes into play when we take a glance at the way in which the happy introvert devises his action plan, which differs, qualitatively and quantitatively, from the way anybody else does it.

As I have indicated time and again throughout this book, introverts prize 'alone' time. We find ways to carve out numerous moments in the day, during which we may commune with our Higher Power, contemplate our navel or, more mundanely, trim our cuticles. When planning snacks or meals, we consciously pick foods and beverages that allow us to indulge our senses, savor our choices, and that leave us feeling energized, content, and ready to tackle the rest of the day (or at least the afternoon). We take alternate routes to and from work, the gym, the park, our relatives' houses, and on our way to weddings, bar mitzvahs, and circumcision celebrations (yes, we Jews actually rejoice at the sacramental removal of a bit of flesh), all in an attempt to end up pleased with the imprint that we permit the world to leave on our being.

In short, we methodically and carefully plan our way through the day, looking at life and living, not as a line, but, rather, as a playing field, within which we have a slew of soul-enriching choices to make. And we make those choices in a deliberate fashion, doing our best to consistently veer towards a convergence of interactions with people, places and things that tickle our deepest fancy. We customize our choices to fit our personal preferences, and rarely, if ever, sacrifice the values we hold close and dear, in exchange for some soporific or fleeting sense of short-lived pleasure. Introverts crave weighty and worthwhile gratification. Nothing less will fill our existential cup.

Are you hungrily seeking a way of being and doing that which concords beautifully with your most passionately held values, goals and interests? Are you consistently dancing on the edge of the sublime? Or are you just showing up on the highway of life and wondering why you keep getting run over? If I ever get stranded, I know which road on which to hitch a ride. Deep down, I think you do, too.

CHAPTER 25

U nless you are intimately familiar with the common character traits of an introvert, you are likely to be very surprised to know that I earn part of my keep as a motivational speaker.

Motivational speakers deliver equal measures of information and entertainment – what I fondly refer to as 'infotainment' – to audiences, small and large. I have been privileged to speak at teachers' conventions, small business association gatherings, and even did a stint in Washington, DC, offering pithy aphorisms and uplifting affirmations about life and living to the members and staff of Congress.

Something weird and wonderful comes over me when I morph into my inspiring and engaging stage presence. I become funny, sharp, and incisive. I get looks from the audience implying that each person thinks I am talking only to them. I am often told, afterward, that this or that participant never met anyone like me, someone so present and alive, someone so magnetic in appearance and delivery. I eat it up.

But, later, I sit there, in the quiet of my hotel lounge, well ensconced in an overstuffed easy chair, and practically hidden from view by a giant fish tank, populated by bug-eyed, splendidly endowed, tropical sea creatures, and I ponder the question: Who in Heaven's name are they really talking about?

It's not that I am not funny, sharp or incisive. Indeed, I am. It's not that I am neither inspiring nor engaging. To the contrary, these are two of my finest attributes. It's not that I have any trouble conveying presence and mindfulness to a group of avid listeners; these may be two of my greatest strengths.

Here's the dilemma: If you were to run into me at a party (unlikely, as I despise them), a small group gathering (it's possible, but, again, the odds are against it), or, perhaps, at PTA night (far more likely, as I am usually the shoo-in for that job, based on my rapport with my seven boys' teachers), and if you had heard about all the marvelous qualities that people attribute to me when they heard me speak in a large group setting, you would swear that you had made a terrible mistake, and were talking to the wrong person.

One-on-one, I am fine. No, scratch that. One-on-one, I SHINE. In very large groups (and, especially when I am leading that group), I am 'THE BOMB.' But put three, four or five people in a circle, including me, and bring up a light and breezy topic, well, I am just plain stumped about where to begin! If there is an entry point into that conversation, it will elude me like a seasoned horsefly skillfully dodges a swatter. I am awkward, jagged, and have great difficulty appearing cogent. I usually end up being the silent observer for a time, then ineffectually bowing out, limply excusing myself (or simply leaving the group without so much as an "I'll be back in a bit") and heading out in an earnest search for the maraschino cherry that unceremoniously toppled from the English trifle, set atop the buffet table, moments ago. Hopefully, that preternaturally discolored, fruity treat will turn up in the diametrically opposite corner of the room from where the aforementioned conversation was being held, and from which I most recently extracted myself. Any measure that would ensure closure, and that would permanently forestall the need to return to that social torture test, would be a welcome relief.

Now I have made you privy to my social modus operandi, I trust that you will exercise all due caution and care when you consider how to involve me in your next soiree. It's simple; either ask me to be the keynote speaker, or make sure that you invite a very close friend of mine with whom I can converse freely throughout the night, avoiding all those other untoward, unnecessary, and potentially embarrassing ***tete-a-tetes*** that tend to populate such gatherings. Alternately, keep a good supply of maraschino cherries on hand. You've been warned.

CHAPTER 26

I drive for Lyft. For those of you who may not know what I am talking about, Lyft is a taxi service, similar to Uber. The potential passenger downloads the app, then clicks on 'need a ride' when the occasion arises, and - presto! - the driver gets an alert on his or her phone that the rubber needs to hit the road. Becoming a driver for Lyft is as easy as uploading one's driver's license and insurance information. For me, it was a no-brainer, largely because I love to drive, but, more importantly, because I am the consummate introvert. Allow me to explain the relationship between the two.

Driving for Lyft is an introvert's paradise. It affords the driver an opportunity to engage in some of the most bizarre, exhilarating and unexpected one-on-ones that a person could ever hope to encounter. We already know that singular interactions are the 'meat and potatoes' of an introverted existence, second only to time alone, and I feel uniquely indebted to Lyft for the platform they have provided, within which I have been able to, fully and exhaustively, exercise my introverted chat muscles.

Driving for Lyft lights up so many bulbs on my introverted switchboard, I don't even know where to begin when describing the pleasure derived from the experience. Not only do I get to engage, person-to-person, with a supremely colorful assortment of peculiar, eccentric and uncommon individuals, but, when the mood strikes, I can also turn off the app, turn up the radio, and rock with abandon to the deafening strains of Guns 'n Roses or Judas Priest. I would never give myself permission to do this if I had no good reason to be in the car in the first place.

Alternately, I can pull over and sit, quietly and anonymously, amidst the urban decay that is Baltimore City, checking my email or posting a photo of yet another open-air drug transaction taking place only a few yards away. The possibilities are only limited by one's imagination.

I can drive to my favorite kosher dining spot, order a bagel with cream cheese (vegetable or chive flavored, *s'il vous plaît*) and a large dark roast, then chill out in the restaurant's dark, deserted recesses, as I wait for my next Lyft page. The owner and I are on a first-name basis, and she understands that she will periodically need to keep my breakfast warm for me, such as when I need to run to pick up a passenger before my meal is ready. I always make sure to pay her in advance, as there have been those days, albeit few and somewhat far between, when the Lyft passenger's destination is on the other side of the planet, and I am unable to make the return trip - my myriad of other, non-Lyft related obligations beckoning - once I am done with that ride. I would never stiff her, even when I am unable to take possession of my southwestern breakfast crepe, as I value her friendship (she's a fellow introvert) and I cannot afford to be the recipient of the 'hairy eyeball' award, should I fail to fulfill my end of the customer-proprietor agreement.

Perhaps the most enticing and intriguing part of being a Lyft driver, though, is that I NEVER know where I am going, after picking up the passenger, until I actually pick them up! Bear with me as I flesh this out, because this notion could, on the surface, appear to run counter to all that predictability and calm that go hand-in-hand with the introverted personality.

First of all, Baltimore is much more aptly known as a big town, rather than a small city. As such, there is virtually nowhere in the vicinity that a Lyft passenger will want to go, and with which I am unfamiliar. I have lived in this area for forty years and can find my way from point A to point B practically blindfolded (my children will sometimes even comment that this is, indeed, how I appear to drive). Therefore, predictability is not under suspicion.

Secondly, the novelty of discovering an as yet unexplored nook, cranny or crevice of the Baltimore landscape and surroundings is delightfully appealing to my introverted brain. It fills my explorer's cup without having to leave the comfort of no more than a fifteen-minute ride to the nearest, clean, convenient rest stop (bathrooms matter). I get to see promising, urban renewal up close and personal (and I also get to recoil with dismay and disgust at horrific urban decay). In short, I become the intrepid traveler, sightseeing on someone else's dime, never too far from civilization as I know and understand it, and operating with the comforting knowledge that even the smelliest, most annoying, and most belligerent passenger is rarely more than twenty minutes away from vanishing in front of my very eyes. Like I said, this is an introvert's version of Heaven without having to die to get there.

Before all of you register to drive for Lyft, however, please understand that this chapter was not underwritten by them, nor is it, in truth, designed to sway your choice of employment. I stumbled upon the opportunity quite by chance, when I realized that most part time jobs that offer $20 per hour require some training, while Lyft only requires the ability to accelerate, steer and stop. I am a simple man. I am pragmatic man. And, most of all, I am an introverted man. As a result, and speaking only for myself, this kind of work can only be described as 'up-Lyfting.'

CHAPTER 27

When I was young, unlike many school-age children, I dreaded summer. In sharp contrast to those who loved sleeping in, and enjoying endless hours of play in the warm sunshine, I pined for Labor Day to come as soon as possible, knowing that I would be returning to the safety of the classroom. The obvious question that comes to mind (after, "What is he, nuts?") would be: What is it about a classroom that connotes safety for this particular introvert? And the answer is that structure and stability equaled predictability – a safe environment for us 'inward' types.

Most kids love to be at ease, unfettered, and given the freedom to find their fun as it arises. Not me. I was a planner from day one. I liked to know what was happening, when and where it was taking place, who was going to be there, and what time we were getting home. I would beg my mom to make reservations for events or playdates, secure in the knowledge that my day would have an order, substance and familiarity to it. I needed to know that the beginning, middle and end were well scripted in advance. Introverts don't necessarily have a lock on this particular compulsion, but we covet it with a vengeance.

An hour at the roller rink was good; I knew all the songs they played over the scratchy loudspeaker, and looked forward to the moments when the announcer would reveal the type of round to come, be it solo, partners, or freestyle. I always ordered the baked pretzel with mustard and an iced tea at the grimy cafeteria, shakily making my way, skates and all, to the unsmiling cashier – her name was Marge – a tight-lipped gal who bravely, resolutely and glumly manned her station. I was prescient enough to use the 'facilities' at home before arriving and lacing up, knowing full well that the unsavory, unsophisticated 'toughs,' from a few towns away, were lying in wait and ready to blindside any innocent bathroom-going skater upon entry, relieving him of his pocket change and anything else in his possession containing a minimum of bling. In short, I knew my way around the joint.

A hike on an obscure trail at an unfamiliar, mountainside park was bad; I could run out of water, forget the bug repellent, or twist my ankle. It could rain or I could accidentally happen upon a mother bear and her cubs. Worse yet, we could get lost on the way, and end up having to endure the indignity of being dragged along to a dozen yard sales, somewhere between "Where are we?" and home, rather than experience a limited, yet refreshing, taste of the great outdoors. The phrase I feared most was, "Let's just get in the car, drive, and see where we end up." Uh, no thanks, I think I am having a mild case of Legionnaire's Disease and need to rest. After all, school starts in seven weeks.

Summer camp was similarly agonizing, but for different reasons. It was there that I had the first of many encounters with that undesirable category of camper known as 'the bully.'

His name was Jonathan, but we called him Pokey, a nickname with dual and nefarious implications; first, he bore a strong resemblance to Gumby's donkey sidekick, but more like his evil, anthropomorphic doppelganger if there ever was one. And, secondly, his favorite method of turning a relatively fun and cheerful day into a grueling, onerous, torture test, was to sneak up behind an unsuspecting, ill-prepared camper, and viciously POKE him in the ribs. Much to my chagrin and dismay, I quickly became his favorite target. After a few days of this treatment, my nightmares shifted from the garden-variety 'monsters in the closet and under the bed' to "Pokey's gonna getcha if you don't watch out!"

I really cannot tell you how I survived that time in my life. I think I blacked it out, as, to this day, I only vaguely recall that one particular detail that I shared with you, but otherwise remember little or nothing about any summer camp experience. A therapist would probably label me as suffering from PTSD, and I would be hard-pressed to argue the point.

Attending summer camp, and enduring run-ins with Pokey, ended when I was twelve years old. I politely but firmly told my parents that, at age thirteen, I was old enough to cut lawns, trim hedges and weed gardens for pay. And so, I did. But as the summer of my fourteenth year rolled around, I had a strange and unfamiliar itch to stretch my wings again. I wanted a genuine summer experience. I just wanted to do it without offering up my introverted self on the altar of disturbed, dysfunctional, social sacrifice.

Call it Providence, G-d, Universal Intelligence or what you will; some One or some Thing intervened as that summer approached, in the form of a suggestion from the mother of a friend. Her eldest son had spent the previous summer doing something very different from the standard summer fare, spending a month bicycling around some rural or alpine part of the United States with a group of teenagers, with an adult heading up the program. My ears perked up. Did someone say 'bicycling?' Did someone mention 'camping on the go'? Did someone imply that a pre-determined route, replete with known and trusted campgrounds, swimming pools, recreational facilities and challenging, gorgeous scenery, were on the agenda? I jumped at the chance faster than a watermelon disappearing at a Gallagher gig.

And so, began my love affair with summer cycling groups. They were everything I had ever wanted out of a two-month-long school hiatus, and more. I logged well over one thousand miles each summer, visiting New York State, Vermont, New Hampshire, Connecticut, Massachusetts, Maine, Nova Scotia and Prince Edward Island. I traced and highlighted - on my trusty, foldable, regional map (no GPS devices existed back then) - dazzling and striking routes around, over and through hills, rivers and valleys, stopping to cool off in sparkling streams and surprisingly powerful waterfalls. I roasted hot dogs on sticks and boiled spaghetti in a clunky pot, over an open fire. I fended off mildly ferocious, yowling, howling, country hound dogs with my menacing bike pump, and I offered foul-tasting, dehydrated, cycling snacks to local kids, as they stared at the strange parade of helmeted, geared-up, brightly outfitted 'peddlers,' passing through their towns.

More than my cycling escapades satisfied the part of me that craved order and predictability – with a sizable dose of excitement and adventure mixed in – they nurtured, cradled, and supported the introvert within, the part of me that loves to be alone.

Riding a bicycle over rugged terrain, for a distance of fifty or more miles each day, is NOT a time to catch up on gossip with a fellow cyclist. One must put one's powers of concentration, attention and effort into the affair. More often than not, thinking takes a back seat to breathing, pumping one's legs, and getting over the next ridge. One gains a tremendous sense of accomplishment, easily exclaiming upon arrival, "That was an awesome ride! I never thought I could do it – until I did!"

Of course, there is a sense of camaraderie as well. It is difficult to spend a month with the same ten people, sharing tents, cookware, and bathing apparel (I decided that I look awful in a tankini), without bonding to some smaller or larger degree. And that's just peachy for the average introvert, because we derive great benefit from connecting with others at a level of commonality. Long-distance biking is the ultimate complement of yin and yang for the classic introvert, combining lengthy, solitary periods of fiercely demanding, physical exertion with down time spent reviewing the intensely robust and natural experiences of the day.

All of us have a still point; a place inside where we intuitively understand that our life is being lived in a hard-won state of balance and equanimity. For many, this awareness is elusive, and may take years of practice before we are fortunate to arrive at its center. But one thing is certain; when the introvert finds that place inside, where all that alone time that he or she craves combines with just the right amount of intimate, essential interaction, the results are nothing short of magnificent.

Go take a spin. Find your center. Then revel in it. You worked hard for it. Celebrate.

CHAPTER 28

Introverts get a really bad rap in social circles. Early on, many of us, not yet realizing our true tendencies, mistakenly and maladroitly attempt to fit in. The results are often disappointing, at best, and horrifying at worst.

There's a great scene in the movie, *Anchorman 2*, starring Will Ferrell and Steve Carrell, where the two of them are standing around the television studio, shooting the breeze with a few other guys. One of them tells a joke, whereupon each of the others laughs and points out why, in their view, the joke was funny. Steve Carrell, the consummate, nerdy introvert, looking dumbstruck and clueless, nonetheless guffaws heartily and exclaims "I don't even know why I'm laughing!"

The moment is not lost on us. Try as we may, we often find ourselves contributing an array of non-sequiturs, bonehead comments, and squeamishly embarrassing faux pas to a conversation. We are not necessarily desperate to be liked, but we nevertheless comprehend, all too well, that man is a social animal, and that blending in with certain groups of people – personal, professional, religious, etc. – can go a long way toward assisting us in achieving a modest level of self-esteem and status.

For better or worse, though, we cannot do it the way everyone else does it. It just doesn't work.

It can take years, even decades, making the same, humiliating attempts at discourse, before we finally realize that we are different, even a bit odd, and hard-wired in an entirely alternate fashion. Accepting ourselves as such is the first step toward healing and growth. Writing about it can be powerful and cathartic. When my fingers started hitting the keyboard on this topic, my initial intention was to only create a diary or blog. But what poured out of me, like a torrent, became the book that you are now reading.

As an observant Jew, I dedicate a portion of my time each day to acquiring a working knowledge of the intricacies of Jewish thought and practice. A large part of my religious study involves looking deeply into the stories told in the Five Books of Moses (also known as the Torah or Pentateuch), and deriving an understanding about how to live life in a purposeful way, using examples from the lives of our forefathers as a template.

The story of Abraham speaks to me, time and again. Known as the father of the Jewish people and an archetype of kindness, Abraham was the progenitor of monotheism. At a time when the world was largely pagan, worshipping a panoply of deities, and behaving rather poorly in the process, Abraham was putting two and two together, from the earliest of ages, ultimately arriving at the awareness that there is but one Creator.

Abraham first realized that G-d was singular rather than plural when he was only a child. As he grew up and older, he married, relocated and had children. Adding to his breadth and depth of experiences offered him the opportunity to revisit and refine his perception of the universe, as presided over by an all-powerful entity.

Periodically, as Abraham would look back on his life, and reflect on what he had learned throughout his journeys, he was able to discern certain truisms. The first was that all creation had a Creator behind it. The second was that this Being wanted to have a relationship with each of us. The third was that G-d had no desire to see us develop into some cookie-cutter version of Himself; quite the contrary. While He certainly desired that we make ourselves over in His image, He also gave us free will, AND an individualized, specialized, custom-made toolkit, designed to provide maximum assistance in actualizing our singular and particular purpose. Our job is to put these tools to use in a way that helps us become our most authentic selves. This means being placed in situations that are, quite frequently, uncomfortable, stressful and challenging, but that are exclusively tailored for our very own personal growth and development. Once we accept the assignment, we must respond in kind, rise to the occasion, and tackle these situations with all of our skills and talents. The reward is a level of self-awareness and self-acceptance that cannot be garnered in any other way. Abraham, having mastered this medium, used every life experience to gain insight into how his strengths, talents and skills would best be used to serve the world, and help to bring it to a state of greater perfection.

As an introvert grasps the notion that his life will contain a series of events, interactions and circumstances that have been masterfully orchestrated by an infinitely kind, just and loving Creator, then he can finally relax, breathe deeply, and begin to enjoy the garment called his personality, one that has his imprimatur embedded in every seam, crease, and cuff. He is finally at home in this vessel called 'self,' and can begin to actively manifest his true reason for being here on this planet.

When it comes down to it, we're really not here all that long. There is much work to do, much responsibility to take on, and much obligation to fulfill. The happy introvert grabs his goggles and fins, then carefully, and with great deliberation, dives into the swimming pool of life. You may not get splashed by him all that often, though, because he tends to do his homework, and only 'suits up' during the hours when aquatic activity is least desirable to others. If, however, you peek out of the door of the locker room, and into the wading area, you may get a glimpse of this magnificent, retiring creature. Better yet, take a look in the mirror after a few laps; he might be staring right back at you.

CHAPTER 29

There's a famous television commercial that was released in the late 1970's. It came to be known as the "Mikey Commercial," and it was about a kid who was very picky, and who wouldn't eat ANYTHING; anything, that is, except for Life cereal. His brothers could only stare in astonishment as Mikey heartily dug in, happily munched away, and devoured a bowl of some new and different breakfast offering that they - his big, tough, daring brothers - had, heretofore, been reluctant to even sniff at.

In some ways, introverts are like Mikey's brothers, but in other ways, are like Mikey himself. Like his siblings, introverts may, at times, exhibit mild bravado, yet are wary when it comes to trying new things. We prefer, instead, to let others forge a path, then stride in and take a stroll when the trail is a bit more well-worn and clear-cut. On the other hand, we trust our senses; like Mikey, we are very picky, but when we intuitively grasp that a particular situation or activity would jibe well with our likes and aptitudes, we ease into it rather readily. I would like, once again, to offer an example from my own life in order to drive this point home.

When I was a junior in high school, like many my age, I was in the midst of anxiously mulling over which college to attend upon graduation. The 'well-worn path' approach held great appeal. I was morbidly averse to the notion of visiting a bunch of unfamiliar schools, even those that promised to deliver a sterling education, and which matched my supposed present and future interests.

Honestly, at age seventeen, what did I really know about what I wanted to do with my life? You could have paraded me around several dozen campuses, from the Mississippi to the Rockies, and back around to the tawny grounds of any east coast Ivy League institution, and I would be as, or even more, clueless when I finished my tour as I had been at the start. I knew so little about myself that trying to pick between one august set of hallowed halls and another would have been as oppressive and counterproductive as deciding on what to eat from a fancy French menu, when all I had ever tasted, up until that point, was fast food-joint hamburgers and fries.

That is why I am forever indebted to Sol Pachinski* (name changed). Sol (as in Solomon the Wise) was the smartest, nerdiest, and most diligent student that has ever walked on G-d's green earth. Sol knew the 'ins and outs' of every overachieving university within five hundred miles, and was vocal when expressing his opinions about each one, especially at lunchtime, where he could be easily overheard by those around him. One fine day, a crowd had gathered, eager to absorb Sol's tidbits of institutional insight, and I, on that day, as luck would have it, was conveniently stationed only one table away.

As Sol proceeded to pontificate on the profusion of choices, elucidating each one's finer points as well as its shortcomings, one option grabbed my attention more than any of the others, and would not let go: The Johns Hopkins University, located in Baltimore, Maryland.

Why did this school beg my consideration? There were, indeed, a bunch of equally desirable selections from which to choose. Why would I forego an opportunity to look into Brandeis, Brown, or Bryn Mawr? Why would I overlook Princeton, Yale or Swarthmore? The East Coast, as we all know, is home to academic greatness, and any one of these outstanding establishments would have readily fit the bill and satisfied my hunger for intellectual excellence. Not every one of them, however, catered to my idiosyncratic and eccentric nature.

The best way to understand how I chose the school I did is to review some of what we have come to know and love about the dear introvert in all of us.

On the whole, we are deliberate, wary, and are not typically thrilled at the prospect of trying out new and different things. My radar and antennae were on high alert when it came to deciding on where to live and learn, after spending almost eighteen, small-town years under the same roof as my parents. The scholastic station I would choose needed to have elements of familiarity and sameness that would comfort, soothe, and support the fragile transition from high school boy to campus man. One yardstick by which I would be able to measure the acceptability of my decision would depend on that school's ability to satisfy my deep-seated need for a mildly fluky, yet readily recognizable, outcome. I was looking for quirky, yet mundane; odd, yet conventional; exciting, yet calculable. In short, I was open to newness, but not to a lot of surprises. The Johns Hopkins experience met these criteria.

Introverts also enjoy returning to the well of fellowship. It is gratifying to engage in a safe measure of wanderlust, yet still manage to connect with faces and places that are original, yet eerily known, and knowable. Baltimore was a natural next step in my educational and environmental evolution, as it hosted a very large, Jewish community, one of the more sizable ones on the East Coast. When the overwhelming diversity of campus communion became too much to bear, escape to a bagel shop or pastrami-saturated deli was well within reach, a stone's throw by bicycle or cab, and home to a taste, smell and décor that was intimate and comfy. I would quickly discover that I had managed to create a 200-mile barrier between me and my former life, while never once leaving my backyard.

In addition, I discovered that the greater Baltimore area, outside the confines of a campus, was tailor-made for the introvert's pleasure and development.

A big town, much more so than a small city, Baltimore boasted of dozens of culturally, ethnically and demographically exclusive enclaves. Without having to battles one's way through maddening crowds, densely packed streets or noisy watering holes, one could easily stumble upon a fantastic assortment of one-of-a-kind stores, shops and stands. Greektown had remarkably dark and smoky grottoes, offering generous samples of exotic foods not found anywhere within a thousand miles of Athens. Fells Point offered a bounty of bars, hippie clothing havens and ice cream vending outlets, all vying for one's attention, while, just a few feet away, seagulls dive-bombed the murky waters of the Chesapeake Bay, angling for a zesty morsel of blue crab that might be carelessly skittering along the surface of the dockside depths. Yuppies flocked to the understated Mount Washington Tavern, located in the neighborhood of the same name, for a late night wild greens and pomegranate seed salad, accompanied by one's choice of twenty or more local beers on tap. And Washingtonians, sick of the hubbub and drone of political rhetoric or non-stop construction in their own precincts, would descend on the abundance of outdoor cafes, tiki bars and seafood bistros that dotted the landscape from north to south.

The town was, and is, a low-rent, low-profile, low-tide delight, an underrated gem that fills an introvert's emotional, interpersonal and spiritual gas tank with hi-test, hi-octane, low-residue revival. Extroverts don't spend a lot of time in this town; there's just not enough going on for them. The lack of high anxiety, interminable congestion, and inhospitable noise leaves them cold. But for those of us who know an underpriced bargain when we see one, Baltimore is truly home to the no-nonsense, 'leave me to my own devices,' 'open your windows and welcome the humidity' collection of quaint, funky, kooky and aberrant oddballs.

To answer your question, yes, I know a few good realtors. Just give me a tiny bit of advanced notice and I'll set you up. See you soon.

Made in the USA
Columbia, SC
13 March 2019